THE

FIELD & STREAM

Firearms Safety
Handbook

The *Field & Stream* Fishing and Hunting Library

HUNTING

The Field & Stream *Bowhunting Handbook* by Bob Robb

The Field & Stream *Deer Hunting Handbook* by Jerome B. Robinson

The Field & Stream *Firearms Safety Handbook* by Doug Painter

The Field & Stream *Shooting Sports Handbook* by Thomas McIntyre

The Field & Stream *Turkey Hunting Handbook* by Philip Bourjaily

The Field & Stream *Upland Bird Hunting Handbook* by Bill Tarrant

FISHING

The Field & Stream *Baits and Rigs Handbook* by C. Boyd Pfeiffer

The Field & Stream *Bass Fishing Handbook* by Mark Sosin and Bill Dance

The Field & Stream *Fish Finding Handbook* by Leonard M. Wright, Jr.

The Field & Stream *Fishing Knots Handbook* by Peter Owen

The Field & Stream *Fly Fishing Handbook* by Leonard M. Wright, Jr.

The Field & Stream *Tackle Care and Repair Handbook* by C. Boyd Pfeiffer

THE
FIELD&
STREAM
Firearms Safety
Handbook

Doug Painter

Illustrated by George De Crosta

THE LYONS PRESS

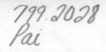

Dedicated to
The International Hunter Education Association
and
the over fifty thousand volunteer instructors
in the United States and Canada

Copyright © 1999 by Doug Painter

Illustrations by George De Crosta

Printed in the United States of America

10 9 8 7 6 5 4 3 2 1

Library of Congress Cataloging-in-Publication Data

Painter, Doug.
    The Field & stream firearms safety handbook / Doug Painter.
       p.   cm. — (Field & stream fishing and hunting library)
    Rev. ed. of: The hunting & firearms safety primer. c1986.
    ISBN 1-55821-912-9
    1. Hunting—Safety measures.   2. Shooting—Safety measures.
3. Firearms—Safety measures.   I. Painter, Doug. Hunting &
firearms safety primer.   II. Title.   III. Title: Firearms safety
handbook.   IV. Title: Field and stream firearms safety handbook.
V. Series.
SK39.5.P34   1999
799.2'028'3—dc21   99-13206
                                                              CIP

Contents

Foreword

Growing up in the hills of West Virginia, I had the opportunity to hunt and handle firearms at a very early age. By the time I was six, I knew how to shoot a .22 rifle and never missed a chance to hunt squirrel or rabbit near my home in Hamlin. During the season, I'd be in the woods at first light and usually have three or four squirrels in a couple of hours. When I got home, I'd skin them and leave them in a bucket of cold water for Mom to cook up for dinner. Sometimes I got so caught up in trying to outsmart a grey squirrel, I was late for school and got hauled over the coals by the principal.

A career in the Air Force didn't slow down my hunting one bit. Wherever I was posted, I often ended up right in the middle of some of the best hunting in the world. Over the years, I've had the opportunity to hunt everything from stag and boar in West Germany's Black Forest and red-legged partridge in Spain to wild sheep in the mountains of Pakistan. Nowadays, I hunt as much for the exercise and the chance to get out with my sons as for the sport. But in a lifetime of hunting, the only thing that has never changed is my attitude toward safety. Whenever I have a gun in my hands, whether I'm sheep hunting up in the high country or just out for an afternoon of skeet, I never forget that safety always comes first.

It's the same attitude I've maintained in over 40 years of flying, whether on a routine mission or during an all-out test of an experimental aircraft. Once in the cockpit, you have no one to rely on except yourself. And, in that sense, safety in the air and safety in the field are much the same. Both demand your full attention. And there's never an excuse for carelessness or recklessness in either.

As much as I've flown, I'm always learning something new. In fact, I don't know a really good pilot who thought he, or she, knew it all. That's good advice for any hunter. There's simply no reason for arrogance in the air or in the field, especially when it comes to safety.

I've been interested in airplanes since I first trained in a P-39 fighter. With each aircraft that I flew, I wanted to know what it could, or couldn't do and why. Before I flew any plane, I really studied the pilot's handbook. When I was done, there was nothing about the aircraft's systems I didn't know. As a hunter, that's how I feel after reading Doug Painter's book. As I see it, it's a real "pilot's handbook" for the hunter, whether novice or veteran. It not only contains the facts that you need to know, but also takes a hard look at the mental attitude that's so much a part of safe and responsible gun handling.

Some of the most pleasant and exciting moments in my life have been in the cockpit of a plane or in the field with a shotgun or rifle in my hand. But I've never forgotten that there's a serious side to both endeavors. You can't expect to get by without doing your homework. And for the hunter, I can't think of a better place to start than with *The* Field & Stream *Firearms Safety Handbook.*

—General Chuck Yeager, U.S.A.F., Ret.

THE
FIELD & STREAM
Firearms Safety Handbook

Willy Yocam and the Monster Buck

The work had gone quickly on Saturday, and by late in the afternoon they were nailing the last of the plywood panels onto the rafters. It was then that it had happened. Willy couldn't remember why he had stopped nailing all of a sudden, or why he had looked up, his gaze landing just over the peak of the roof. But when he did, standing not 80 yards away at the edge of the clear cut where the power line had gone through was the largest buck he had ever seen. His rack was awesome: massive symmetrical beams that curved backward, then out and forward. Willy was sure that he counted twelve points.

The buck didn't seem to notice him at all. He stood at the edge of the clearing for a few moments, then trotted across the open ground to the woods beyond. Willy almost fell off the roof.

When Willy finally got down, he could hardly get his words out straight.

"You wouldn't believe it; you just wouldn't believe it."

"Believe what? You came down from the roof like you'd seen a ghost."

"Biggest buck I've ever seen. Biggest damn deer anyone's seen around here. Just standing up there in the power line cut like he was king of the world."

Sitting there on the tailgate of Mickey's pickup, they made plans for opening day. The land around the ski house was owned by the ski resort, and Mickey was one of only a handful of men who had permission to hunt the property. They both knew that was a big advantage. On opening day there wouldn't be an army out

1

there pushing deer all over the place, especially into the really thick stuff. No, they figured, if luck was on their side, that buck just might stick to his daily pattern. "That old orchard," Mickey had said, "it can't be more than 50 yards beyond the power line. I'd bet anything that's exactly where the ol' rascal is heading every night. Never knew a deer that could get his fill of apples."

It never crossed Willy's mind that Mickey might try to shoot the monster buck. Mickey just wasn't like that. Hell, Mickey rarely shot bucks at all. Most every season, he ended up taking a nice fat doe on his antlerless permit. "The meat's a whole lot better," he would say, "and, anyway, I'm usually back home watching the ball game while the rest of you guys are still out here freezing your tails off."

Willy made Mickey swear that he'd tell no one about the buck. "I'm not even going to tell my wife," Willy told him.

Even though it was still pitch black outside, Willy didn't need his alarm to wake up on this morning. The day had finally arrived. He'd been dozing on and off since three, listening to the steady drum of the rain during the times he was awake. The rain, unusual for this late in the year, had tapered off to a drizzle by the time he left the house to meet Mickey. A good omen, Willy thought. The woods would be quiet. Lousy weather for the skiers, but great for us.

Mickey was waiting when he pulled up in front of the Judd Mountain ski house. Over coffee in the cab of Mickey's truck, they went over their strategy one last time: Mickey would follow the logging road around to the north side of the mountain. From there, he would crest the ridge and start working his way down the south slope. Once at the base, he would start a slow zig-zag pattern, working his way west back toward the ski house.

Even if the buck had changed his pattern, Mickey believed the deer was still bedding down in the thick brush at the base of the mountain and, with a little luck, he could push him toward the power line cut.

Willy's job was easier. He had selected a stand at the base of an old red oak on a small knoll about 50 yards down from the house. From there, he had a clear view of the cut, especially the spot where the buck had appeared a few days ago.

"Well, Mickey," Willy said as he got out of the truck, "I sure hope this works."

"Relax, this one's in the bag. Just you be ready when that buck steps out under the wires."

"Don't worry about that. I'll have my eyes glued to that spot all day."

Even in the darkness it didn't take Willy long to find the oak he'd chosen for his stand. He was confident that nothing would happen till later in the day, but just in case, it didn't hurt to be ready at first light. Actually, Willy never did mind the hours of waiting on a deer stand. By the time the sun came up, he always had the feeling that he'd somehow become a fixture of his chosen corner of the woods. Even on this damp and chilly morning, it was a snug, secure feeling. Of course, Willy realized that just standing there, trying to move around as little as possible, was about as close as you could come to doing nothing. But it was doing nothing with a purpose.

Looking down, he could see that it was a good year for acorns. His father would have liked that. Dad had never been much of a deer hunter, but had dearly loved to go after squirrel. When Willy was twelve, his father had bought him a single-shot, bolt-action .22. It had a knob on the end of the bolt that you had to pull back before the gun would fire. Anyone can pump the woods full of lead, he remembered his father saying. Waiting and watching, son, that's what real hunting is all about. You sit there just as still as you can be, and sooner or later curiosity will get the best of most any bushytail. He'll eventually poke his head out and then come sneaking around to your side of the tree. And when he does, one shot is all you need.

It took Mickey three hours to come over the mountain and work his way down the south slope. The land leveled out at the base of the ridge, but here, the hardwoods gave way to dense thickets interspersed with stands of short pine. Whitetail heaven, Mickey thought. There could be a hundred deer in this stuff, and I'd never see a one. They'll be sneaking past me like I was wearing a blindfold.

Once he was sure of his bearings, Mickey began to head west, stopping occasionally to break the pattern of a steady walk and always angling back and forth to cover as much ground as possible.

Around three-thirty, the rain picked up again, a steady, cold drizzle. Willy had stuffed a poncho in his pack but didn't dare make a move to put it on. There was only an hour of daylight left. Time was running out. "Come on, come on," he whispered to himself. "Where the hell are you?"

Willy was cold, he was tired, and he was getting edgy. Just standing there, trying not to move a muscle, had become an ordeal. Now, it was all he could do to concentrate, to keep his eyes focused on the power line. Had that buck somehow got wind of him? Was he just standing back in the edge of the woods waiting till dark to come out?

No, Willy reassured himself. That's a crazy thought. But right now I'd give anything to know for sure. "Damn," he said softly, "if only something would happen."

Mickey was sure he was somewhere close to the ski house. Not much farther he thought, and I'll be out of this mess. During the past hour he had heard several deer and caught a glimpse of two does as they disappeared into the pines. But whether Willy's buck was still in front of him, had circled back around, or, for that matter, was in the area at all, he had no idea. Nor did he really care anymore. At this point, he could only think of how good a few beers and a thick steak at Pat's would taste.

Another squirrel? No, the noise seemed too loud and too steady. Without trying to move his head, Willy scanned the power line. Where was that sound coming from? Yes, there it was, just below the big clump of brambles about halfway up the cut. For a moment, he was sure that he saw something move through the tightly packed gray birch. That ol' rascal, Willy thought; he's waiting till the very last minute. Willy's grip tightened around his rifle, and he carefully eased the safety off. For Willy, time seemed to stop.

"You wouldn't have believed it," he could hear himself say to the guys later that night at Pat's. "Only a few minutes of light left and, all of a sudden, there he was. A grand, last-minute appearance. But you guys know how it is with these monster bucks. They don't get that way by being dumb."

"They sure don't," Bob would say. "And, I'll say right now that's the biggest buck taken in this country in more than a few years. He'll top 250 pounds easy."

For a few seconds, Willy could see only a dark mess, but then the deer began to take shape. He was hardly moving, walking with his head down, likely on the trail of a doe. Willy didn't remember bringing his rifle up, but he could feel the damp stock pressed to his cheek. His sights centered just behind the big buck's shoulder. He could hardly breathe. "Squeeze the trigger," he said under his breath, "pull it off nice and easy."

The bullet from Willy's 30-06 struck Mickey on his left side just below his fourth rib. Mickey Ringold was pronounced dead on arrival in the emergency room of the Dorville Memorial Hospital at 6:38 p.m.

CHAPTER

Hunting Accidents:
Causes and Types

U NTIL THE DAY Willy shot his best friend, he had every reason
to believe he was a safe hunter. After all, like most of his
friends, Willy had grown up with guns. He had hunted since
he was 10, first with a .22 for squirrels and rabbits and, when he
turned 14, had started going after deer. During the past nine seasons,
he had taken six nice bucks. Where Willy lived, handling a rifle, like
driving a tractor, was something you just naturally grew into at an
early age. Not that he had now become careless: Willy had a healthy
respect for his 30–06 and knew exactly what it could do. Guns were
simply not something you fooled around with, no different really than
the big 10-inch cut-off saw Willy often used on site. You had to watch
what you were doing every minute of the way.

Accidents? Well, they always happened to someone else.

Indeed, most veteran hunters view hunting accidents with a similar
sense of skepticism. The classic reaction, for example, to any mistaken-
for-game accident goes something like this: "I just can't understand
how anything like that happens. I mean, how could any hunter who
isn't half-blind actually mistake a man for a deer in the woods?" The
implication is, of course, clear. We assume that it takes a true incompe-
tent, a real idiot, to make that kind of awful error—someone who has
likely spent little or no time in the woods and is the kind of "hunter"
who might also shoot a cow or goat thinking it was a whitetail.

While this attitude is understandable, it is far from correct. In large
measure, the opposite is true: Most mistaken-for-game incidents actually involve experienced hunters, typically mature men with more
than five years of hunting experience. Indeed, veteran hunters are

7

more likely to be involved in all accident types in which there is an intentional discharge. And as often as not, the victim in a hunting accident is a close friend or family member. As much as hunting accidents are personal tragedies for all involved, they also become statistics such as these, facts and figures that can provide a better understanding of what causes accidents in the field, which, in turn, can help us all become safer hunters.

To begin with, most hunting accidents aren't really accidents at all, at least not in the sense of being chance misfortunes. Unavoidable circumstances or just plain bad luck are rarely, if ever, contributing factors. What, then, is involved? An analysis of yearly hunting accident reports from throughout the country underscores a distinct and familiar pattern to hunting accidents from one season to the next. The same mistakes are repeated each year, with almost all accident cases falling into relatively few categories both as to cause and type.

Indeed, four categories account for close to 50 percent of all hunting accidents each year, including about 45 percent of all accidents that result in a fatality. Each accident in these categories involves an intentional discharge.

1. Victim was out of sight of the shooter.
2. Victim was mistaken for game.
3. Victim was covered by a shooter swinging on game.
4. Victim moved into line of fire.

A common thread runs through all these categories: Accidents in each involved a critical judgment error in a "shoot/don't shoot" situation. The abundance of these accidents underscores the impact of attitudes and emotions as major contributing factors to hunting accidents. Hunters who place a tremendous importance on success in terms of game bagged, who are highly competitive in the field, who are easily frustrated, or who may become overly anxious and excited are far more likely to make snap judgments, to pull the trigger before giving sufficient consideration as to whether or not a shot is safe.

Accident reports also reveal that some 33 percent of all accidents are self-inflicted. However, when those accident categories in which the possibility of a self-inflicted injury is impossible or unlikely are eliminated, the percentage soars to over 60 percent. The risk of a self-inflicted injury—or fatality—is extremely high in the following categories:

1. The shooter stumbled and fell.
2. Someone carelessly handled a firearm.
3. The trigger caught on an object.
4. Someone removed a firearm or placed a firearm in a vehicle.
5. A firearm fell from an insecure rest.
6. A firearm discharged in a vehicle.
7. Someone crossed an obstacle improperly.

The common denominator among these accident types should be obvious to every hunter. In each case, an accident occurred either because a fundamental safety rule or safety law was violated, or a proper gun-handling procedure was not followed. There is nothing complicated here, but these statistics reinforce the concept that accidents almost always are caused by some hunter's mistake, whether through carelessness, ignorance, or lack of skill in handling a gun.

Accident statistics confirm that the safety record of hunting continues to improve, even though hunter density in many areas has increased. In the early 1980s, for example, total accidents averaged more than 1,600 a year. Almost 20 years later, annual accidents had dropped to an average of 1,100. Similarly, in this time frame the average number of annual hunting fatalities has decreased from 222 to 99.

One big reason for this decline has been the tremendous growth of hunter-education programs throughout North America. Today, some three quarters of a million young hunters receive instruction in the safe and responsible use of firearms each year. Courses are sponsored by various wildlife agencies in all 50 states and all Canadian provinces. Most programs include a minimum of 12 hours of instruction, and many states and provinces offer advanced programs of study. Every hunter in North America owes a vote of thanks to the International Hunter Education Association and the some 60,000 volunteers involved in hunter-safety education. Thanks largely to their efforts, many serious injuries have been avoided, and many lives have been saved.

The widespread use of fluorescent orange clothing is another major reason for the decline of hunting accidents, especially line-of-sight incidents. States with mandatory fluorescent (hunter) orange laws have typically been able to reduce these types of accidents by half, sometimes by as much as three-quarters. Today, the use of hunter orange is mandatory in 40 states.

Though significant progress has been made in reducing hunting accidents throughout the country, there can be no room for complacency. Too many accidents still occur. They almost always result in a serious injury, and some 10 percent of all accidents are fatal. Whether we are novice or veteran hunters, there are still lessons to be learned, new perspectives on the subject to be gained.

To be sure, hunting and firearms safety is not a subject of choice. As hunters, we'd much rather read about misty mornings in the duck blind; great dogs and fine double guns; perhaps share in the experience of a Yukon sheep hunt or maybe pick up a few tips on how to find more grouse and keep our dogs working in close. Yet as hunters, we can never forget that safety must always be our foremost concern.

How Does This Gun Work?

On a narrow shelf about three-quarters of the way up from the floor and running the full length of each wall in the L-shaped bar sat some three dozen decoys, mostly divers, but with a sprinkling of blacks and mallards, each an old working block now retired from active duty. Beneath the shelves, hung in a haphazard array, were mostly old waterfowling photographs: hunters, with well-worn doubles or Winchester 97s, standing next to Model A Fords, both draped with countless ducks and geese; Labs and the occasional Chessie lined up in formal pose; even a few grainy stills of the long-outlawed punt guns, their cannonlike barrels jutting past the bows of narrow, shallow draft skiffs.

A martini? No, Cal Lockhart thought: bourbon, with just a splash of water. This place was exactly as it was supposed to be—not some New York designer's interpretation of sporting ambiance.

"So, you think the birds will be flying tomorrow morning?" the man sitting next to Cal asked without introducing himself.

"Sure hope so," Cal replied. "It's my first time here."

"I've heard all the theories," the man continued. "Rain, fog, snow, sleet . . . storm front moving in, or just going out. Phase of the moon, you name it. To tell you the truth, all those guides can say what they want. I think it's just a matter of luck. The geese either come in, or they don't. You do much hunting?"

"Oh, when I was a kid," Cal said. "A few rabbits, a squirrel or two. That sort of thing. It's been a lot of years, though. Don't really have much time for it anymore."

"No need to worry," the man said as he got up to leave. "It's a lot like riding a bike. Once you get back on, it all comes right back."

The skid blind had been pulled to the middle of a large field, some 25 acres of now-harvested corn and 20 more in soybeans still drying on the stalk. More than 100 decoys, a combination of goose silhouettes and shells, had been set out around the blind the night before. Cal and his hunting partner, Ken Trombley, arrived at six-thirty in the morning.

"Well, you think they'll be flying today?" Ken asked just after they had settled into the blind.

"From what I heard in the bar last night," Cal came back, "no one really knows for sure."

"I see you're learning fast," Ken said. "How about a cup of coffee?"

Ken Trombley had leased the farm for the entire season, an expensive proposition, but one he hoped would pay good dividends. Cal Lockhart was his biggest client.

By eight o'clock, it was obvious that it was not going to be a classic waterfowling day. Though the temperature remained in the high 30s, there was no wind and just a few high, wispy clouds: real bluebird weather. Over the next few hours, the men did see a flight or two, but the geese were off in the distance and flying high. By eleven, not even the blackbirds were flying.

Ken was upset that they hadn't even come close to getting a shot that morning. "Listen, nothing will be up and moving till late afternoon," he said. "Why don't we go back to the inn for a bowl of snapper soup and maybe a few crab cakes?"

"Sounds good," Cal replied, "but don't worry about me. I'm having a great time just sitting right here."

"No phone, no messages, no meetings. I know what you mean," Ken replied, feeling relieved. "I'll tell you what: let's have some lunch and then we'll come right back out."

Cal's shotgun was in front of him, standing upright, the barrel resting in a notch cut into the 2 by 4 that braced the blind. It was a 12-gauge pump he had borrowed from Ken for the weekend. Cal picked up the gun, ready to unload before leaving the blind.

"You all set?" Ken asked, opening the plywood board that served as a door to the blind.

"I will be as soon as I get the slide to go back. Seems to be stuck."

"No, you have to first pull back on that metal catch on the trigger guard. Then you can pump the shells out."

Cal tried to get a good grip on the serrated edge of the catch with his gloved hand, but, as he pulled, his finger slipped. The blast inside the blind was deafening. The load of high brass No. 2 shot blew a jagged hole in the side of the blind and then struck one of the shell-bodied decoys, sending it cartwheeling through the corn stubble.

After a moment of stunned silence, Ken said, "Good lord, Cal, I didn't know you wanted a goose that badly."

Cal Lockhart just sat where he was and didn't say a thing. On top of everything else, he realized he'd never put the safety on. Or perhaps he'd pushed it off when he had mounted the gun to get the feel of it that morning? Of one thing he was sure: There was nothing, absolutely nothing, funny about what he had just done.

Firearms and Ammunition

OMMON SENSE and early experience had led Cal Lockhart to do the right thing: unload before he left the blind. But it had been a long time since he'd had any practice. In fact, Cal hadn't touched a gun in over 20 years. To be sure, that's not an everyday example, but it's not unusual for many hunters to handle their equipment only a few times each year.

Being familiar with your gun—and knowing what it's capable of doing—is the first and most basic step in becoming a safe hunter. That point seems obvious, but it's surprising how often it's overlooked. Each season, more than several hundred accidents occur when guns are simply being loaded or unloaded.

First of all, if you lend a gun to a friend, always take a few minutes to explain and demonstrate the key features of that particular firearm. For example, be sure that the person who'll be using your gun knows:

- How the action works.
- How to properly load and unload the gun.
- How to operate the safety switch.
- What ammunition should be used.

The same advice holds true for any gun that you own. Whenever you buy a new gun, for instance, don't neglect to go over the instruction manual that comes with it. (If you bought a used gun or did not receive an instruction booklet with your new gun, write to the manufacturer for the appropriate manual. They'll be happy to send you one.) Getting acquainted with a new gun the morning of opening day can be not only frustrating, but can also be dangerous. So, before you shoot that new gun:

- Be sure you have followed all instructions for assembly, if required. Conversely, do not disassemble the gun beyond the point the manufacturer recommends.
- Be sure you understand how the action works and how to properly load and unload the gun.
- Be sure you know where the safety switch is and how it works.
- Be sure you understand the steps involved in cleaning your gun. Before loading the gun, make absolutely sure that the inside of the barrel is free of dirt or other objects. Even a small obstruction can result in a serious injury. Never try to remove an object from the barrel by loading another cartridge or shell and firing.
- Be sure you know what is the proper ammunition for your new gun. **Ammunition must be in the same caliber or gauge as that marked on the firearm by the manufacturer.** It's a good idea to carry only the proper ammunition for the gun you are shooting. A 20-gauge shot-shell, for example, will pass through the chamber of a 12-gauge and lodge in the barrel. So, whenever you head out, check the pockets of your hunting coat or vest to be sure you are carrying only the ammunition specifically intended for the gun you're using.

If you lend a gun to a friend, always take a few minutes to explain and to demonstrate the key features of that particular firearm: how the action works, how to properly load and unload, how to operate the safety, and what ammunition should be used.

Whenever you buy a new gun, don't neglect to go over the instruction manual that comes with it.

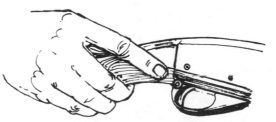

Before you shoot any gun, be sure you know the location of the safety and how it works.

When it comes to matching ammunition with a firearm, "close" is never good enough. The Sporting Arms and Ammunition Manufacturers' Institute (SAAMI) reminds us that "The firing of a cartridge or shell other than that for which the firearm is chambered can result in the cartridge or shell rupturing and releasing high pressure gas that can damage or destroy the firearm and kill or seriously injure the shooter and persons nearby."

Certain dangerous ammunition and firearm combinations are easily recognizable, but many also have similar chamber and cartridge dimensions. There are countless dangerous combinations; however, SAAMI has developed an extensive list of specific unsafe arms and ammunition combinations.

Rimfire rifle

IN FIREARMS CHAMBERED FOR	DO NOT USE THESE CARTRIDGES
.22 WRF	.22 BB, .22 CB .22 Short .22 Long .22 LR .22 LR Shot
.22 WMRF	.22 BB, .22 CB .22 Short .22 Long .22 LR .22 LR Shot
.22 Win Auto	.22 BB, .22 CB .22 Short .22 Long .22 LR .22 LR Shot
5-mm Rem RF Magnum	.22 BB, .22 CB .22 Short .22 Long .22 LR .22 LR Shot .22 Win Auto
.25 Stevens Long	5-mm Rem RF Magnum

Shotgun

IN SHOTGUNS CHAMBERED FOR	DO NOT USE THESE SHELLS
10 Gauge	12 Gauge
12 Gauge	16 Gauge
12 Gauge	20 Gauge
16 Gauge	20 Gauge
20 Gauge	28 Gauge

IN SHOTGUN CHAMBERED FOR	DO NOT USE THESE CENTERFIRE METALLIC CARTRIDGES
410 Bore	Any

With any gauge, shot shells of a given nominal length should not be fired in a gun the chamber length of which is shorter than the fired shell length; for example, a 3-inch (75-mm) shell fired in a 2 ¾-inch (70-mm) chamber.

Centerfire Pistol and Revolver

In firearms chambered for	Do not use these cartridges
9-mm Luger (Parabellum)	9-mm NATO (Military) .40 S&W 9 × 18 Makarov
9-mm Win Mag	9 × 18 Makarov
9 × 18 Makarov	9-mm Luger .38 Auto .38 Super Auto .380 Auto
.32 H & R Mag	.32 Long Colt
.32 S&W	.32 Auto .32 Long Colt .32 Short Colt
.32–20 Win	.32–20 High Velocity
.38 Auto	.38 Super Auto +P* 9-mm Luger
.38 Super Auto +P	9-mm Luger 9 × 18 Makarov
.38 S&W	.38 Auto .38 Long Colt .38 Short Colt .38 Special 9 × 18 Makarov
.38 Special	.357 Magnum .380 Auto
.38–40 Win	.38–40 High Velocity
.40 S&W	9-mm Luger
.44–40 Win	.44–40 High Velocity
.45 Auto	.38–40 Win

*+P ammunition is loaded to a higher pressure, as indicated by the +P marking on the cartridge case headstamp, for use only in firearms especially designed for this cartridge and so recommended by the manufacturer.

Centerfire Pistol and Revolver (continued)

IN FIREARMS CHAMBERED FOR	DO NOT USE THESE CARTRIDGES
	.44 Rem Magnum
	.44 Special
	.44–40 Win
.45 Colt	.38–40 Win
	.44 Rem Magnum
	.44 S&W Special
	.44–40 Win
	.454 Casull
.45 Win Mag	.45 Auto
	.454 Casull

Centerfire Rifle

IN FIREARMS CHAMBERED FOR	DO NOT USE THESE CARTRIDGES
6-mm Remington (244 Rem)	.250 Savage
	7.62×39
6.5-mm Remington Magnum	.300 Savage
6.5×55 Swedish	7-mm BR Remington
	7.62×39
	.300 Savage
7-mm Express Remington	7-mm Mauser (7×57)
	.270 Winchester
	.30 Remington
	.30–30 Winchester
	.300 Savage
	.308 Winchester
	.32 Remington
	.375 Winchester
	.38–55 Winchester
7-mm Mauser (7×57)	7.62×39
	.300 Savage
	.30–30 Win
7-mm Remington Magnum	7-mm Express Remington
	7-mm Mauser (7×57)

Centerfire Rifle (continued)

In firearms chambered for	Do not use these cartridges
	7-mm Weatherby Magnum
	8-mm Mauser
	.270 Winchester
	.280 Remington
	.303 British
	.308 Winchester
	.35 Remington
	.350 Remington Magnum
	.375 Winchester
	.38–55 Winchester
7-mm Weatherby Magnum	7-mm Express Remington
	7-mm Mauser (7 × 57)
	7-mm Remington Magnum
	8-mm Mauser
	.270 Winchester
	.280 Remington
	.303 British
	.308 Winchester
	.35 Remington
	.350 Remington Magnum
	.375 Winchester
	.38–55 Winchester
7-mm-08 Remington	7.62 × 39
8-mm Mauser (8 × 57)	7-mm Mauser (7 × 57)
	.35 Remington
8-mm Remington Magnum	.338 Winchester Magnum
	.350 Remington Magnum
	.358 Norma Magnum
	.375 Winchester
	.38–55 Winchester
.17 Remington	.221 Remington Fireball
	.30 Carbine
.17–223	.17 Remington
	.221 Remington Fireball
	.30 Carbine

Centerfire Rifle (continued)

In firearms chambered for	Do not use these cartridges
.220 Swift	7.62 × 39
.223 Remington	5.56-mm Military .222 Remington .30 Carbine
.240 Weatherby Magnum	.220 Swift .225 Winchester
.243 Winchester	7.62 × 39 .225 Winchester .250 Savage .300 Savage
.25–06 Remington	7-mm BR Remington 7.62 × 39 .308 Winchester
.257 Roberts	7.62 × 39 .250 Savage
.257 Weatherby Magnum	.25–06 Remington .25–35 Winchester 6.5-mm Remington Magnum .284 Winchester 7-mm-08 Remington 7-mm Mauser 7.62 × 39 .308 Winchester .300 Savage .303 Savage .307 Winchester .30–30 Winchester .32 Winchester .32–40 Winchester .35 Remington .350 Remington Magnum .356 Winchester .358 Winchester .375 Winchester .38–55 Winchester

Centerfire Rifle (continued)

In firearms chambered for	Do not use these cartridges
.264 Winchester Magnum	.270 Winchester
	.284 Winchester
	.303 British
	.308 Winchester
	.350 Remington
	.375 Winchester
	.38–55 Winchester
.270 Weatherby Magnum	.25–06 Remington
	.270 Winchester
	.284 Winchester
	7-mm-08 Remington
	7–30 Waters
	.30 Remington
	.30–30 Winchester
	.308 Winchester
	.300 Savage
	.303 Savage
	.307 Winchester
	.32 Winchester
	.32 Winchester Special
	.32–40 Winchester
	.35 Remington
	.35 Remington Magnum
	.356 Winchester
	.358 Winchester
	.375 Winchester
	.38–55 Winchester
.270 Winchester	7-mm Mauser (7 × 57)
	7.62 × 39
	.30 Remington
	.30–30 Winchester
	.300 Savage
	.308 Winchester
	.32 Remington
	.375 Winchester
	.38–55 Winchester
.280 Remington	7-mm Mauser (7 × 57)
	7.62 × 39

Centerfire Rifle (continued)

IN FIREARMS CHAMBERED FOR	DO NOT USE THESE CARTRIDGES
	.270 Winchester
	.30 Remington
	.30–30 Winchester
	.300 Savage
	.308 Winchester
	.32 Remington
	.375 Winchester
	.38-55 Winchester
.284 Winchester	7-mm Mauser (7 × 57)
	.300 Savage
.30–06 Springfield	7.62 × 39
	8-mm Mauser (8 × 57)
	.32 Remington
	.35 Remington
	.375 Winchester
	.38-55 Winchester
.30–40 Krag (30 Govt)	.303 British
	.303 Savage
	.32 Winchester Special
.300 Holland & Holland Magnum	8-mm Mauser (8 × 57)
	.30–06 Springfield
	.30–40 Krag
	.375 Winchester
	.38-55 Winchester
.300 Savage	7.62 × 39
.300 Weatherby Magnum	.338 Winchester Magnum
.300 Winchester Magnum	8-mm Mauser Rd. Nose Bullet
	.303 British
	.350 Remington Magnum
	.375 Winchester
	.38-55 Winchester
.303 British	.30–30 Winchester

Centerfire Rifle (continued)

IN FIREARMS CHAMBERED FOR	DO NOT USE THESE CARTRIDGES
	.32 Winchester Special
.303 Savage	.30–30 Winchester
	.32 Winchester Special
	.32–40 Winchester
.308 Winchester	7.62 × 39
	.300 Savage
.338 Winchester Magnum	.375 Winchester
	.38–55 Winchester
.340 Weatherby Magnum	.350 Remington Magnum
	.375 Winchester
	.38–55 Winchester
	.444 Marlin
.348 Winchester	.35 Remington
.375 Winchester	.38–55 Winchester
	.41 Long Colt
.378 Weatherby Magnum	.444 Marlin
	.45–70 Government
.375 H&H Magnum	.375 Winchester
	.38–55 Winchester
.38–55 Winchester	.375 Winchester
	.41 Long Colt
.416 Rigby	.416 Remington
.416 Weatherby Magnum	.416 Remington
	.416 Rigby
	.45–70 Government
.460 Weatherby Magnum	.458 Winchester

Be sure you know what is the proper ammunition for your gun. Ammunition must be in the same caliber or gauge as that marked on the firearm by the manufacturer.

GUNSMITHING

Working on guns is very much like working with electricity. In either case there is no room for guesswork. If you're still at the "let's give it a try" stage, you'll most likely get yourself into trouble. At best, you might end up with a gun that doesn't work. At worst, your handiwork can turn a gun into a truly hazardous piece of equipment. Sure, go ahead and reshape and refinish a stock, touch up the blueing, or add a recoil pad or swivels and a sling, but stay clear of modifying or in any way altering the basic firearm, *especially* any work that involves adjusting the trigger or changing the shape or size of the sear, sear notch, or any other parts in the trigger assembly. It's also a point to keep in mind when buying a used gun. Was the former owner an amateur gunsmith? Have any of the critical parts of the gun been altered? If you're not sure, don't take a chance. Have the gun looked over by a qualified gunsmith. It's cheap insurance.

The same advice holds true for any gun—whether it's an old double-barreled shotgun from your grandfather or a deer rifle you picked up for a bargain price—that you have the slightest doubt is in

If you have the slightest doubt that a gun is in good working condition, have it looked over by a qualified gunsmith.

good working condition or is safe to shoot. Outward appearances can be deceiving: the proper engagement of key internal parts, such as sears and hammers, may have been affected by old oil and grease that's turned to varnish or simply by many years of wear and tear.

How Far Will Your Gun Shoot?

Shotguns

How many times have you watched a flight of geese come over just a bit too high for a clean shot or sat helplessly by as the ducks came in 25 yards beyond the outer edge of your rig? The fact is, situations such as these keep reminding all of us who hunt with shotguns that they are effective at only relatively short range.

There is, remember, another kind of range that you must be familiar with: *the maximum range your shot load will carry.* From a safety standpoint, this knowledge is equally important.

Indeed, whether you're a duck and goose hunter or a grouse and woodcock hunter, *you should never forget that the maximum effective range of your load is always substantially less than the maximum distance the shot charge will travel.*

The following are the approximate maximum horizontal distances for the leading pellets of shotstrings fired from a 12-gauge shotgun.

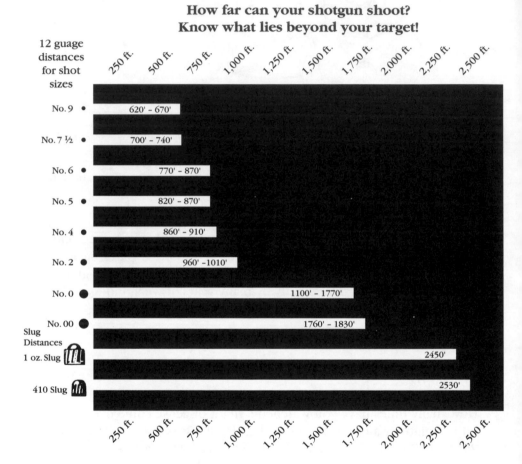

How far can your shotgun shoot?
Know what lies beyond your target!

12 guage distances for shot sizes

| | 250 ft. | 500 ft. | 750 ft. | 1,000 ft. | 1,250 ft. | 1,500 ft. | 1,750 ft. | 2,000 ft. | 2,250 ft. | 2,500 ft. |

No. 9 • 620' – 670'

No. 7 ½ • 700' – 740'

No. 6 • 770' – 870'

No. 5 • 820' – 870'

No. 4 • 860' – 910'

No. 2 • 960' –1010'

No. 0 ● 1100' – 1770'

No. 00 ● 1760' – 1830'

Slug Distances

1 oz. Slug 2450'

410 Slug 2530'

Many countries in the more populous and built-up areas of the East and the South require deer hunters to use shotguns, either with buckshot or rifled slugs, instead of centerfire rifles. The reasoning behind this requirement involves a basic safety consideration: the maximum distance a 12 gauge, 1-ounce rifled slug will travel is about one-fifth the maximum distance of a popular deer caliber such as a

30-30. A load of 12-gauge buckshot has an approximate maximum distance about 200 yards less than the rifled slug.

While these shotgun loads will travel significantly shorter distances than centerfire bullets, the point to always remember is that they can travel far beyond your target. The effective range, for example, of a 12-gauge slug is in the vicinity of 100 yards—yet that slug can travel over 800 yards.

So whenever you're in the field, whether you're hunting waterfowl, upland game, deer, or are just out for an afternoon of informal clay target shooting, *always think along the lines of a "safety zone" in all directions of fire.*

- Where, and how far away, is your hunting partner? In which direction, if any, would a shot at a low-flying bird be safe?
- If you're practicing with clay targets, do you have a safe background of at least 300 yards?
- Are you familiar with the area where you hunt?
- Is there a new vacation home just beyond your favorite grouse covert?
- How about farm buildings, livestock or roads in the vicinity of your deer stand?

It's your responsibility to know the answers to questions such as these whenever you head out. And, if you're even in doubt—*don't shoot.*

Rifles

Exactly the same logic applies to rifles, even more so. Indeed, instead of thinking in terms of feet, with rifles it's a matter of miles. The bullet from a 30–06, for example, one of the most popular and time-tested of all big-game calibers, can travel almost 4 miles, even farther at high elevations. By any standard, that's a long, long way. Even a .22, minuscule by comparison to a 30–06, should never be underestimated. A high velocity .22 long rifle pushes a 40-grain solid-point bullet out of the barrel at 1,255 feet per second and develops 140 foot pounds of energy at the muzzle. It will travel its first 100 yards in 0.26097 seconds. Velocity at 100 yards will still be at 1,016 feet per second, and at 200 yards the bullet will still be traveling at 893 feet per second. And a .22 has a maximum range of over a mile and a half. That's over 2,200 yards—22 football fields laid end to end.

The following chart provides the maximum range of a variety of popular rimfire and centerfire cartridges.

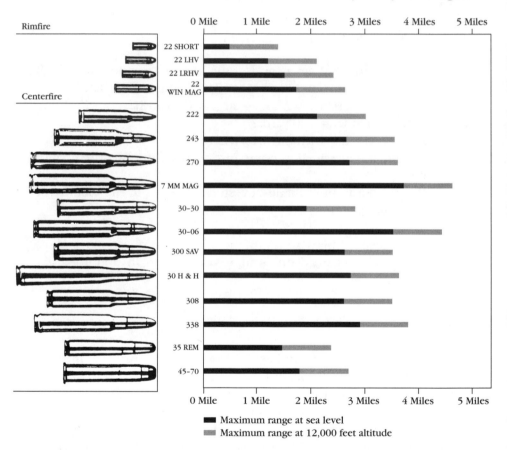

**How far can your rifle shoot?
Know what lies beyond your target!**

Again, the underlying safety point is that you must be fully aware that the bullet from your rifle, whether a .22 or a 30-06, can travel a very substantial distance beyond your target. Never take a shot unless you have a safe backstop or you are absolutely sure of what lies in the area beyond your target.

CHAPTER

One Careless Moment

To Art Sorensen, the true measure of seasons past was not in the years, but in his dogs. Each dog, beginning with Czar in '47, had for him become a distinct and separate block of time, a well-defined cycle of seasons and memories—some short, others long—every one an era unto itself.

Now in his 68th year, he was once again starting a new era: his ninth dog, 'Maggie,' a young springer spaniel, a gift from his long-time hunting partner and neighbor, Tyler Metcalf.

With each new dog there was always a wonderful sense of anticipation. What would this one be like? Yet for the first time his joy was tempered by the thought that she just might be the end of the line, his last hurrah.

"I sure hope she's a good one," he said when Tyler had first brought her over to the house that summer.

"Don't you start thinking like that," Tyler had kidded him. "That's exactly why I gave 'Maggie' to you. I figure the only way for an old-timer like you to stay young is to spend your time chasing after a flushing dog."

"Tyler, what I really like about you is the way you're always looking out for me."

Art and Tyler had been members of the same pheasant club for the past 20 years. Nothing fancy, just an old clapboard clubhouse with some kennels out back and about 150 acres of land, mostly in old pasture that was cut back every few years, and a few fields planted in short sorghum. It was a perfect place to work the dogs. Plenty of good cover and an unlimited supply of birds. "I don't care about a dog's so-called potential," Art had often told Tyler. "If you

31

don't shoot a whole lot of birds over him, he'll never amount to much."

Art let down the tailgate of his old Wagoneer. "Okay, young lady, show Tyler here what you can do." "Maggie" was out before he had finished, running tight circles around him, nose to the ground. It was warm for late September, so Art had planted only half a dozen birds. A quick morning's workout, he told Tyler, just something to get our hearts started.

Not 50 yards out, "Maggie" ran by her first bird, wheeled around when she picked up the scent, and came crashing back through the sorghum. The cock bird got up, pumping hard for altitude. Art was still some 30 yards back. He saw tailfeathers with his second shot, but the bird didn't go down.

"He's hit, but not hard. I've got him marked. Glided down the hill toward the swamp."

"Where'd the dog go?"

"Where do you think, Art? She took off after that bird the moment you shot. She's got to be at the bottom of the hill by now."

"Thanks for the backup, Tyler."

"Old buddy, since when did you need me to do your shooting?"

"Yeah, I know. Should have stayed up closer to her. Thought she was just working off a little steam. I didn't plant our birds in this field."

"Well, Art, maybe when she gets older, she'll know which birds are ours."

"Okay, wise guy. I'll go on down and see what she's up to."

It was a steep and slippery climb down the hill and even tougher going down below. It had been many years since he and Tyler had pushed the swamp for holdover birds. Now, he remembered why. You either slogged your way through the muck or jumped from one grass hummock to another.

Art fell twice before he finally crossed the swamp and reached drier ground. He hadn't yet spotted "Maggie," but he knew the going would be easier along the edge. He was upset that she'd taken off after the bird but, then, what young dog wouldn't have? About 40 yards down, he spotted her. She was sitting at the base of a long-dead hickory, her eyes fixed on the pheasant that was perched high on one of the bare branches. He knew there was only one thing he could do. The shot from his 20 gauge dropped the cock pheasant instantly, and "Maggie" was on the bird in a flash. "Good girl, good girl," he said, as "Maggie" came over and dropped the bird by his feet.

Art realized he'd been gone almost half an hour, and he pushed himself to get back. By the time he reached the top of the hill, he was breathing hard and his light canvas shirt was blotched with perspiration. Tyler was where he had left him, seated on an old stone wall, smoking his pipe.

"Well, 'Maggie,' from the looks of him, you'd think he was the one doing all the work."

Art was too tired to say a thing. His back hurt, and he could feel the chill in his legs from his wet pants. He sank down next to the wall and propped his shotgun up alongside him.

"Okay, young lady," Tyler said, "let's take a look at your first bird."

Art struggled to pull the pheasant from his game pocket and then flipped it over to Tyler. "Maggie" lunged for the bird.

The shot was deafening.

In the next few weeks, neither Art nor Tyler could remember whether it was the dog or one of them that had knocked the gun over, not that it really made any difference.

In any case, Art considered himself lucky. He lost only three toes from his left foot.

CHAPTER

Playing by the Rules

S OME HUNTERS simply don't know any better; others think the rules were written for someone else. A few are just downright reckless. Art Sorensen certainly knew better than to lean a loaded gun against a wall. As a rule, he was a careful and conscientious gun handler and had hunted without incident for over 30 years. What happened? In Art's case, the real culprit was fatigue. He had become tired to the point of being exhausted, and for one brief moment he had stopped thinking. The result? A careless and very dangerous mistake.

Accident statistics show that accidents classified as "gun handling" or "safety rule violations" are most likely to occur among very young hunters, and those who are older, typically 55 and up. Among the former, lack of skill and lack of familiarity with guns is often a major contributing factor. Among the latter, fatigue typically plays a major role. In each and every case, however, the accident happened because a fundamental rule of safe hunting or safe gun handling was ignored.

Take a moment and read through the following accident reports selected at random from a variety of state accident summaries. Each is presented as written by investigating authorities.

- Victim decided to cross fence. He threw gun over his back; gun discharged and went into his back and buttocks.
- Shooter asked victim if gun was loaded. Victim answered no. Shooter picked up gun with his finger in the trigger guard. The shotgun discharged, and the blast hit the victim in the stomach.
- Victim was running through the forest when gun went off and hit him in the leg. He did not know the gun was loaded.

- Victim was running toward a wild hog when gun leaning against a tree fell from its resting place and gun discharged—hitting victim in the back.
- Victim stated that he had leaned the shotgun against the left side of the Bronco and sat in the driver's seat. He saw shotgun slide down the side of the Bronco and hit the door jamb and the gun went off.
- Victim was a passenger in an airboat which had stopped. While stopped, victim was feeding dog, lost his balance and fell onto loaded gun he was holding. Rifle discharged striking victim in the forearm and left side of stomach.
- Shooter was walking toward victim when he tripped and his rifle fired. The 6mm soft core bullet struck victim in the right bicep. He bled to death before reaching a hospital.
- Shooter was walking behind victim. Uncocked his 410 shotgun and hammer slipped. Gun discharged, striking victim in the back of his leg at the knee.
- Subject hunting rabbits, put muzzle of his rifle on foot and unintentionally pulled trigger.
- Subject hunting rabbits in heavy brush and firearm got hung up in bush, trigger caught on branch, firearm discharged into victim's stomach.
- Subject hunting partridge. In process of turning around, he accidentally pulled trigger and shot himself in right foot.
- Victim hunting rabbits. Walking 30 feet ahead of shooter. Victim crouched down, looking for tracks. Shooter stumbled and fell at same time and gun accidentally discharged, striking victim on left side of stomach. Shooter charged under Criminal Code.
- Victim was about to shoot at ducks on a pond when he changed his mind and started to put his gun down. The gun went off, striking him in the leg.
- Shooter struck tree with butt of his gun in an attempt to scare a squirrel. His gun discharged: the shot struck the victim in the shoulder.
- Victim was climbing a tree with his shotgun. He fell, the gun discharged and the shot struck the victim in the chest.
- Victim was riding in an All Terrain Vehicle with his shotgun resting between his legs. He hit a bump and the gun discharged. The shot struck him above the right knee.

- Victim was using the butt of his loaded shotgun to clear limbs from a tree. The gun fired on impact; the shot entered his upper body.
- Shooter was jumping on a brush pile . . . the gun went off, striking him in the left foot.

Bizarre circumstances? A once in a million sequence of events? A freak accident? Pure chance, or plain misfortune? Hardly: Accidents such as these didn't just happen. Each was caused by some hunter's mistake. All, and many others like them, could have been avoided. It's a point that can't be emphasized enough.

Whenever you pick up a gun, no matter what the circumstances—whether you're excited or relaxed, tired or anxious to get going, whether you're cold, wet, frustrated, feeling disappointed, or just wishing you were back home in front of the fire—you can never forget . . . not even for a moment . . . that handling your gun in a safe and responsible manner should be your first and foremost concern.

Whenever you pick up a gun, no matter what the situation—whether you're hot on the trail of a big buck or admiring your first grouse of the season, whether you're breaking for lunch in the field or packing up at the end of the day—you can never forget . . . not even for a moment . . . that handling your gun in a safe and responsible manner should be your first and foremost concern.

This may all sound redundant, but safety never is.

Safe Gun Handling, Step by Step

ALL TOO MANY ACCIDENTS occur in and around vehicles, the place where most hunts start and finish.

So to begin with, be absolutely sure your gun is unloaded before you put it in your trunk or the back of your wagon or truck. There's never a good reason to carry a loaded firearm in your vehicle, even if you're just driving a short distance to a new hunting location. You should be aware that having a loaded gun in a vehicle is a game-law violation in most areas; indeed, it's surprising just how many so-called accidents also involve a violation of the law.

Once you arrive at your destination, leave your gun in the vehicle while you get the rest of your gear organized. Some hunters are always in a big rush to get their guns out, and then end up leaning them against the side of the car or truck or other insecure rest such as a fencepost or tree—invariably where a gun could easily be knocked over or slip. It's a bad habit to get into. Uncase your gun only when you're ready to go, and when you do, keep it unloaded with the action open as you head out. **The only time your gun should be loaded is when you're in the field and actually hunting.**

When you do load, make sure that your next step is to place the safety in the "on" position—and don't take it "off" until just before you shoot. If your target flares or gets out of range before you can get a shot off, don't forget to put the safety back on. While you should never neglect to properly use the safety, neither should you rely on it as fool-proof. As with any other mechanical device, it cannot guarantee safety.

Even when your hands are full, you must pay strict attention to where the muzzle of your gun is pointing.

In some circumstances, if a loaded gun is dropped, the safety may not be sufficient to prevent the firing pin from striking the cartridge or shell and firing the gun. Careless handling can never be excused with the phrase, "Don't worry, the safety is on." One more point about safeties: Keep your fingers away from the trigger while moving the safety, and never pull on the trigger when the safety is engaged.

A very large number of accidents could be avoided each season if all hunters **treated their guns as if they were loaded at all times.** In large measure, this means keeping the muzzle always pointed in a safe direction. **Never point your gun at anything you do not intend to shoot.**

Never assume that any gun is unloaded. Always check yourself to make sure.

Always handle your gun by the stock, whether you're placing it in, or taking it out of, a car, truck, or boat—wherever it might be. Never grab onto a gun by the barrel and pull it toward you or anyone else. Whether you're standing around waiting for your partner to catch up or passing a gun over to a friend—whatever the situation—the moment you pick up a gun, you should start thinking, "Where is the muzzle pointing?" And don't stop thinking about it until the gun is safely put away. This is a cardinal rule of safe gun handling, and it applies to any gun, whether it's loaded or not. **Never assume that any gun is unloaded. Always check yourself to make sure.**

In the field, there's not only the question of muzzle awareness but also the matter of muzzle control. Whenever a gun is in your hands, it's essential that you maintain the ability to control the direction in which the muzzle is pointing. There is more than one way to do this safely and still have your gun ready for quick use. It's largely a matter of choosing the right carry for the right situation.

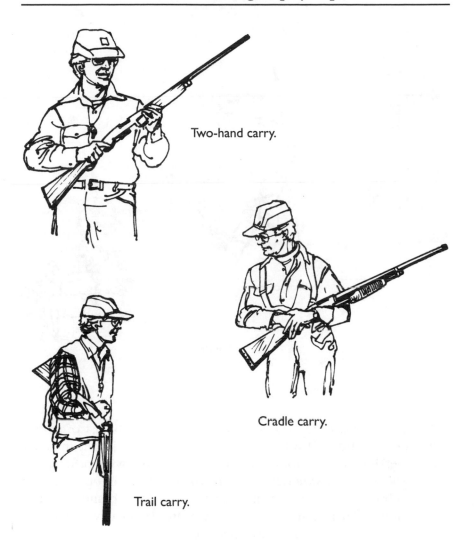

Two-hand carry.

Cradle carry.

Trail carry.

Hunter safety instructors suggest the following:
- The *two-handed* or *ready carry* gives excellent control of the gun and the muzzle. It's safe and, at the same time, allows you to raise your gun for a quick shot.
- The *cradle carry* is safe to use but has one drawback: Since the muzzle is pointed to one side, it should not be used when a person is walking beside you.

Side carry.

Sling carry.

Shoulder carry.

- The *trail carry* is safe to use when walking abreast of several people. It can also be used when you are the leader in single file. However, do not use this carry when following others.
- The *elbow* or *side carry* is safe when walking in open terrain. In brushy areas, however, it's easy for a twig or branch to catch onto the barrel and push it downward. This carry should not be used when hunters are ahead of you.
- The *sling carry* is used by many rifle hunters when walking long distances. This carry has the advantage of leaving both hands free, but should be avoided when moving through thick brush or low overhangs. The muzzle could get caught, causing the rifle to fall off your shoulder.
- The *shoulder carry* is a good choice when walking beside or behind other hunters. A word of caution with this carry: Since the muzzle is out of sight, you must be careful to keep the barrel pointed upward. In any case, this carry should not be used when others are behind you.

In any situation where you might slip or fall, be sure to carry your gun unloaded, with the action open.

Of course, no matter which way you carry your gun, your finger should always be outside the trigger guard and the safety should be "on." A special note when using handguns: Carry a loaded revolver with empty chamber under the hammer. Carry loaded pistols with the magazine inserted but with an empty chamber.

Muzzle control involves knowing when to unload your gun. In the field, there are countless situations in which the risk of losing your balance, of slipping and falling, is simply too great to justify carrying a loaded gun. It might be going down a muddy ditch, making your way up a rocky embankment, or crossing a swampy area or stream or it might be going over an obstacle, such as a fence or fallen tree. In every case, unload your gun—and leave the action open—before you proceed. If you do fall or stumble, be sure to check that your barrel is completely clear of any mud, dirt, or snow.

The same logic applies when moving through dense cover: You don't want to be caught pushing branches out of the way or pulling brambles off your pants with a loaded gun in the other hand.

Obviously, there can't be a rule to cover every potentially danger-

Whenever you encounter an obstacle, such as a fence or fallen tree, unload your gun—and leave the action open—before you proceed. If you should fall or stumble, check that your barrel is completely clear of any mud, dirt, or snow.

ous situation when handling a gun. That's where common sense comes in. When you have a gun in your hands, avoid any action that might cause you to lose control and subsequently point the muzzle in an unsafe direction. Don't run with a gun or jump up and down on a brushpile, for example. And never lean a gun against any part of your body. A gun isn't a walking stick or a support of any kind, and it should never be used as a tool to probe or clear away twigs or branches. These points may seem to be an elaboration of the obvious. Unfortunately that's not the case with all hunters. The proof is in the accident reports written up each year.

Muzzle control applies to all shooting situations in terms of safe zones of fire. Simple in concept, your safe zone of fire is defined by the horizontal and vertical arcs in which you may fire a shot without endangering others. Though we usually think of zones of fire in relation to our hunting partner(s), they also may apply when hunting in areas in which buildings, roads, livestock, or other human activity make shooting in certain directions unsafe. You should be aware of

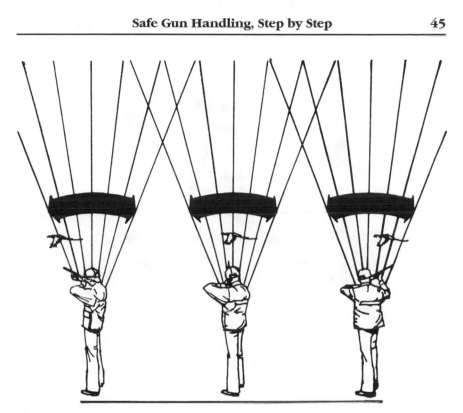

Your safe zone of fire is defined by the horizontal and vertical arcs in which you may fire a shot without endangering others.

any "off-limits" shooting areas where you hunt, and you should be sure to point them out to everyone in your group before you head out. And if you're getting permission to hunt on someone else's land for the first time, be sure to inquire about any "off-limits" shooting areas.

Good planning is the critical ingredient to establishing safe zones of fire. **Never set up a situation in which anyone in your hunting party could inadvertently end up in the line of fire of another. Remember: The vast majority of line-of-sight accidents involve members of the same hunting party.**

The larger the hunting party, the more difficult it is to maintain prearranged positions and movements when in the field. In almost all hunting situations, try to limit your group to no more than three hunters.

If you're walking, start out—and always stay—abreast of each other. With three in a party, the center hunter has all the going-away shots at targets on their respective sides. Never swing "down the line."

If you're walking, start out—and always stay—abreast of one another. Whether there are two or three of you, this straight-line deployment gives each hunter a clear and well-defined zone of fire. With three in a party, for example, the center hunter has all the going-away shots, whereas the hunters on each end have safe shots at targets on their respective sides. In no case should anyone swing "down the line."

Staying "on line" is especially critical when moving through heavy cover or hilly country—any terrain where it's easy to get out of alignment or lose sight of your partner(s). If an obstacle forces you to change your course, let your partner(s) know right away. **You can't know your safe zone of fire unless you know the location of your hunting partner(s) at all times.** If you do lose sight of one another, don't hesitate to whistle or call out to re-establish contact. When visibility is a problem, wearing hunter (fluorescent) orange provides an enormous safety advantage. It's amazing to what degree this high-visibility color can help you spot your partner in the brush and in low-light conditions.

Establishing well-defined zones of fire is equally important when hunting from fixed positions, often the case when hunting dove, pass shooting at ducks or geese, or deer hunting from stands. When selecting sites, each hunter should know in advance his or her safe zone of fire, and if the group is large, one member of the party should coordinate the placement of the entire group. Each hunter should be familiar with his or her assigned spot and the location of everyone else.

When a bird flushes or a rabbit bursts out of a brush pile, for example, you'll often have only a brief second to decide whether it's a safe shot or not. So always keep a clear mental picture of just what

You can't know your safe zone of fire unless you know where your partner is at all times. If you do lose sight of one another, don't hesitate to whistle or call out to reestablish contact.

Establishing well-defined zones of fire is equally important when hunting from fixed positions, often the case when hunting doves, pass shooting at ducks or geese, or deer hunting from stands.

is your safe zone of fire. By constantly thinking ahead and anticipating the kind of shot you might be presented with, you'll know in advance which shots will be safe and which will not be.

During any hunt, there are times when you'll take a break, whether it's just for a few minutes to catch your breath or to sit down for lunch in the field. Whenever you do, be sure that your first move is to unload your gun and leave the action open. Unloaded or not, never prop your gun up or rest it where it might easily be knocked down or slip over.

It's doubtful that many hunters are insomniacs. A day spent crouched in a duck blind or a day spent slogging through the brush in search of grouse takes a lot out of you. Come sundown, the walk back to the car always seems twice as long, and your gun feels as if it's gained a pound or two. It's a potentially dangerous time for every

Whenever you take a break, be sure that your first move is to unload your gun and leave the action open. Never prop your gun up or rest it in a way where it might easily be knocked down or slip over.

hunter. Even if you're in good shape, your coordination and concentration aren't what they were when you started off in the morning. And when you're tired, whether just pleasantly so or downright exhausted, it's easy to become a little sloppy in the way you handle your gun. It's time for extra and deliberate caution. So be sure to double-check your gun to make sure there are no shells in the chamber or the magazine. The hunt isn't over until your gun is cased and safely put away.

If you're a young hunter, you're probably at an age when you're also starting to drive. Getting behind the wheel and handling a gun have much in common. The rules of the road and the rules of gun safety are not complicated. And driving a car or shooting a gun are not especially difficult. Sure, both are something you have to learn and practice. Yet the real key to safe driving and safe gun handling is a matter of concentration. The moment you start thinking about the term paper you haven't finished, the pass you dropped in the end zone, or whether you should ask Mary out for Saturday night, instead of paying attention to the road, is just when you'll drive right past a stop sign or right through a red light. Exactly the same logic holds true when handling a gun. The moment you stop thinking about what you're doing is the moment you realize that your muzzle is pointing right at your partner's back.

When driving or handling a gun, you simply can't allow your mind to wander. Even a small lapse in concentration can have tragic results. And in either case, the responsibility for safety rests entirely on your shoulders.

Once You Pull
the Trigger . . .

Phil Westhoff wasn't sure if the intermittent kee-kee *sounds came from a hen or from a tom, but he was certain that, for the first time in his life, he was listening to a wild turkey. For a few minutes, he thought the calls might be getting closer, but half an hour later they seemed neither louder nor fainter than before.*

Phil had heard how hard it was to sneak up on a turkey, but it was after 10 A.M. and he'd been in the woods since before daylight. Why not give it a shot? He was bored sitting in one spot, and, in any case, this was the only bird he'd heard all day. Trying to make as little noise as possible, he got up and began to head in the direction of the calls. Every few steps, he stopped to listen. The bird, it seemed, was staying put. Another 30 yards or so, and Phil thought he might be within range.

Phil was so startled by the next series of calls that he almost jumped backward. The bird must be just ahead. His first impulse was to make a dash for it. Maybe he could get close enough for a quick shot. No, he knew he didn't really stand much of a chance. But he couldn't just stand there in the open. Getting down on all fours, he inched his way to a fallen tree and, careful not to snap a twig or branch, crouched behind the blowdown.

For a full minute he didn't dare move. Then the turkey called again and, from the sound of it, was now straight ahead and maybe a little to the right. Phil peered over the edge of the log. At first, he could make nothing out; but as his eyes focused farther out, he picked up a flash of red from the turkey's neck. The bird was deep in the undergrowth at the base of a red oak, about 25 yards away.

Phil suppressed the urge to stand up and shoot. Instead, he slowly pushed the barrel of his shotgun across the log and pivoted the gun until the front bead centered on the turkey's neck. His index finger found the safety and pushed it off. The bird seemed to jump straight up in the air. Had the soft click spooked him? Phil froze but kept staring at the spot where the turkey had been.

A flash of gold . . . a hand? What was going on? Had he dozed off for a minute? Was he dreaming? Nothing made any sense. Yet something was there. His eyes raced to complete the puzzle, trying to fit the pieces together. The curve of a man's shoulder . . . legs pulled tightly to his chest . . . a head covered by camo netting. All of a sudden, everything came into focus. It was now all clear as day. There at the base of the oak sat another turkey hunter. Phil watched him wipe his forehead with a red bandana and then tuck it back into his hip pocket.

Phil could feel the air push out of his lungs. His right hand wouldn't stop shaking. My God, he thought, I almost shot you.

Phil couldn't resist looking back toward the tree. He was positive that there had been a turkey right there. But now, he could only see the man. There was no turkey, after all. Only the high-pitched kee-kee *sounds as the other hunter started calling again.*

The Illusion of
Early Blur

PERCEPTION, like beauty, is often in the eye of the beholder.

In our mind's eye we can easily build an image of what we want to see, especially if it's something we expect to come into view. That's precisely what happened to Phil Westhoff. He was out hunting turkey, and his every sense was attuned to that expectation. Whatever he saw or heard in the woods, he was likely going to translate into turkey.

It's surprising just how little information we sometimes need to construct an entirely lifelike mental picture. The initial visual clues may be rudimentary and few in number—a red bandana, a brown hunting coat, an oddly shaped branch, or just the play of light and shadows among the rustling leaves—but all of a sudden, standing there in front of us is a wild turkey or a white-tailed deer. All hunters, no matter how many years they've spent in the field, are susceptible. Indeed, the more we know what to look for, the easier we can be fooled.

As hunters, we are predisposed to see and to hear the game we're hunting. Typically, we've scouted an area and have chosen a location in which game sign is abundant. As a result, we often don't need much coaxing to convince ourselves that game is nearby. The crude form that first catches our eye, perhaps supplemented by a sound or movement, is enough to trigger a mental process wherein our mind's eye rapidly fills in the missing parts of what we anticipated seeing. A patch of brown moving in the brush blossoms into a full-fledged 10-

Researchers recognized that some brilliant color was needed to help hunters stand out instead of blending into their surroundings.

point buck. A red bandana becomes a big tom. The illusion is hardly subtle. Hunters involved in mistaken-for-game accidents often insist that they actually shot at an animal and that the victim somehow appeared and stepped into the line of fire.

The nature of this type of hallucination—the phenomenon of "seeing" what we want to see—was not understood by the hunting community until the late 1950s, when a series of tests were undertaken to determine which color was the most visible against a woodland scene and could help hunters "stand out" instead of blend into their surroundings. The tests, conducted with the cooperation of the U.S. Army, conclusively demonstrated that fluorescent (hunter) orange was by far the most easily seen and recognized bright, unnatural color against a natural background.

During the testing, the researchers became aware of a study on human perception being conducted at Harvard University. In one experiment, the researchers began by showing subjects hopelessly blurred side transparencies on a screen. The images were slowly brought into focus, and the subjects were asked to identify the picture as soon as they could. Although the subjects could eventually identify the image, it was obvious that their perception came well after the point when anyone just walking into the room would have immediately recognized what was on the screen. Apparently, there was something about the early blur of the image that hampered recognition.

To confirm their suspicions, the researchers conducted further tests, this time with two groups of subjects who were shown identical pictures. The first group was exposed to slides that changed slowly from a hopeless blur to a middling point of focus. After the projector was turned off, only 25 percent of the subjects were able to correctly identify the picture. The second group was exposed to the pictures in reverse order, starting from a medium blur and then going farther back out of focus. In this group, 75 percent of the subjects—unhampered by the effects of early blur—were able to shortly recognize the picture.

Perhaps the most revealing by-product of this research involved the significant number of subjects who identified a picture while it was still blurred and then continued to believe their original hypothesis—to still "see" what they had initially only guessed at—even after the picture had been brought into sharp focus.

This study helped prove that hunters were prime candidates for the effects of "early blur." In 1965, one researcher noted that, "Might not the sportsman, his mind attuned to the hunt, his every sense groping for a deer, suffer a like illusion? More than any other individual, the big game hunter often works in the world of early blur. His is the first, pale hour of dawn in the wilderness, and the last blue wash of gathering twilight. He stalks his quarry in the gloom of black growth and in the big cedar swamps where, even at midday, broken shadows and splotchy patches of sunlight confuse vision."

As any veteran hunter of the backwoods whether he's ever seen a deer, only to find, after careful stalking, that the "deer" was a curiously shaped stump or the silhouette of a bush against the sky? Invariably, the answer is "yes."

Over the past 40 years, hunter orange has proved to be an enormously effective deterrent to mistaken-for-game accidents. The color is so bright and so effectively shouts "human-made," that it shatters the illusions influenced by early blur. The color overrides and dispels the visual clues that initially activated our imagination. "One spot of hunter orange," a researcher notes, "and the human mind instantly rejects the formation of a mental deer or game image."

Massachusetts was the first to pass a mandatory hunter orange regulation, requiring Bay State deer hunters to wear no less than 500 square inches of hunter orange clothing. Consequently, dramatic results were achieved in Massachusetts and in other states requiring hunter orange. Indeed, nationwide, few if any mistaken-for-game victims have been shot while wearing hunter orange.

Every hunter should understand that hunter orange is by far the easiest color to see and least likely to be confused with anything in nature. Yellow, for instance, can be seen as white at certain hours of the day, and the once traditional hunter's red can appear as a dull hue to those with color-vision deficiencies. Hunter orange is the only satisfactory color to wear under all weather and light conditions and, in fact, its fluorescence is accentuated during the poor light at dawn or dusk or when the shadows are heavy. Keep in mind that hunter orange clothing will fade and, when it does, it loses a large measure of its effectiveness. So, be sure to replace your vest, jacket, and cap as soon as they've lost their original brilliance.

As important as it is to wear hunter orange (where it is appropriate for the game you're hunting), it is equally important *not* to wear or carry anything that might make you resemble a game animal. When deer hunting, avoid the colors brown and white. When turkey hunting, avoid red, white, or blue.

Evidence to date indicates that deer see in black, gray, and white. We may never know for sure, but it's a fact that hunter success has not declined in those areas where hunter orange is mandatory. When state game officials in Maine first tested the effectiveness of hunter orange, they required its use in only one county. At the end of the season, hunter success in that county had increased, but stayed the same in the rest of the state.

More than 80 percent of the states now have some type of mandatory hunter-orange requirement, and all states strongly recommend its use. You should be knowledgeable about the specific requirements in your state and in any other state where you plan to hunt.

U.S. States and Canadian Provinces Mandating Hunter Orange (as of 1995)*

UNITED STATES

ALABAMA All hunters during gun deer season must wear a vest or cap with at least 144 square inches of **solid** hunter orange, visible from all sides. Deer hunters in tree stands elevated more than 12 feet from the ground need not wear hunter orange, except when traveling to and from tree stands. Only hunter orange, blaze orange, or ten mile cloth is legal. (Exception: waterfowl, turkey, and dove hunters and those hunting legally designated species during legal right time hours.)

ALASKA Upland and big-game hunters are strongly recommended to wear hunter orange.

ARIZONA Upland and big-game hunters are strongly recommended to wear hunter orange.

ARKANSAS It shall be unlawful to hunt any wildlife, or to accompany or assist anyone in hunting wildlife, during a gun or muzzle-loading deer season without wearing an outer garment above the waistline, of daylight fluorescent blaze orange (hunter orange) within the color range of 595 nm–color range of 555–565 nm (hunter safety green) totaling at least 400 square inches, and a fluorescent blaze orange or fluorescent chartreuse head garment must be visibly worn on the head. **EXCEPTIONS:** (1) While migratory bird hunting. (2) While hunting in areas in which hunting of deer with guns is prohibited. **PENALTY:** $50 to $1,000.

CALIFORNIA Upland and big-game hunters are strongly recommended to wear hunter orange.

COLORADO It is unlawful to not wear at least 500 square inches of **solid** (camouflage orange is not legal; mesh garments are legal, but not recommended) daylight fluorescent orange material in an outer garment above the waist, part of which must be a hat or head covering visible from all directions while hunting deer, elk, or antelope during any muzzle-loading rifle or rifle seasons. Bow hunters are not required to wear orange during the archery only seasons.

Source: Highland Industries.

CONNECTICUT No person shall hunt any wildlife from September 1 through the last day of February without wearing at least a total of 400 square inches of fluorescent orange clothing above the waist visible from all sides. This color requirement shall not apply to archery deer hunting during the separate archery season (except on private lands during the muzzle-loader deer season); to archery and firearms turkey hunting; to waterfowl hunters hunting from blinds or a stationary position; to raccoon and opossum hunting from one-half hour after sunset to one-half hour before sunrise; or to deer hunting by a landowner on his own property.

DELAWARE During a time when it is lawful to take deer with a firearm, any person hunting deer in this state shall display on his head, chest and back a total of not less than 400 square inches of hunter orange material.

FLORIDA All deer hunters, and those accompanying them, on public lands during open deer season must wear at least 500 square inches of hunter orange on an outer garment above the waist. (Exception: bow hunters during bow season.)

GEORGIA All deer, bear, and feral hog hunters, and those accompanying them, during firearm deer seasons must wear at least 500 square inches of hunter orange on outer garments above the waist.

HAWAII All persons in any hunting area where firearms are permitted must wear a hunter orange outer garment above the waist, or a piece of hunter orange material of at least 144 square inches on both their front and back, above the waist. A **solid** hunter orange hat is recommended.

IDAHO Upland and big-game hunters are strongly recommended to wear hunter orange.

ILLINOIS It is unlawful to hunt or trap any species, except migratory waterfowl, during the gun deer season in counties open to gun deer hunting when not wearing 400 square inches of solid blaze orange plus a hat. It is unlawful to hunt upland game (pheasant, rabbit, quail, or partridge) when not wearing a hat of solid blaze orange.

INDIANA Deer (bow and gun), rabbit, squirrel, grouse, pheasant, and quail hunters must wear at least one of the following **solid** hunter orange garments: vest, coat, jacket, coveralls, hat, or cap. (Exception: bow hunters for deer during first archery deer season.)

IOWA All firearm deer hunters must wear at least one or more of the following articles of visible **external** apparel: A vest, coat, jacket, sweatshirt, sweater, shirt, or coveralls, the color of which shall be **solid** hunter orange.

KANSAS Big-game clothing requirements: (a) Each individual hunting deer or elk, and each individual assisting an individual hunting deer or elk, shall wear hunter orange clothing having a predominant lightwave length of 595–605 nm; (b) The bright orange color shall be worn as follows: (1) a hat with the exterior of not less than 50 percent of the bright orange color, an equal portion of which is visible from all directions; (2) a minimum of 100 square inches of the bright orange color on the front of the torso; and (3) a minimum of 100 square inches of the bright orange color on the back of the torso.

KENTUCKY Hunter orange garments shall be worn by all deer hunters while hunting on any location on property where any deer gun season is permitted by regulations. Garments shall be worn as outer coverings on at least the head, chest and back. They shall be of a solid, unbroken pattern. Any mesh weave opening shall not exceed ¼ inch by measurement. Garments may display a small section of another color. Camouflage pattern hunter orange garments do not meet these requirements.

LOUISIANA Any person hunting deer shall display on his head, chest, and/or back a total of not less than 400 square inches of material of a daylight fluorescent orange color known as hunter orange during the open gun deer hunting season. Persons hunting on privately owned, legally posted land may wear a cap or a hat that is completely covered with hunter orange material in lieu of the foregoing requirements to display 400 square inches of hunter orange. These provisions shall not apply to persons hunting deer from elevated stands on property which is privately owned and legally posted, or to archery deer hunters hunting on legally posted land where firearm hunting is not permitted by agreement of the owner or lessee.

MAINE Anyone who hunts with a firearm during any open firearm season on deer is required to wear two thirds of **solid-colored** hunter orange clothing (fluorescent orange) which is in good and serviceable condition and which is visible from all sides. One article must be a hat. The other must cover a major portion of the torso, such as a jacket, vest, coat, or poncho. Regulations require that anyone who hunts in the moose-hunting district during the moose season must wear one article of **solid** hunter orange clothing.

MARYLAND All hunters and those accompanying them must wear either (1) a cap of **solid** daylight fluorescent orange color; (2) a vest or jacket containing back and front panels of at least 250 square inches of **solid** daylight fluorescent orange color. Maryland requires 50 percent of camouflage hunter orange garment to be **daylight fluorescent orange color;** or (3) an outer garment of camouflage fluorescent orange worn above the waist which contains at least 50 percent daylight fluorescent orange color. (Exception: Hunters of wetland game birds, fur-bearing mammals, doves, crows, wild turkeys, bow hunters during archery season only, falconers, and unlicensed hunters on their own property.

MASSACHUSETTS All hunters during shotgun deer season and deer hunters during primitive firearm season must wear at least 500 square inches of hunter orange on their chest, back, and head. (Exception: waterfowl hunters in a blind or boat.) All hunters on wildlife management areas during pheasant and quail season must wear a hunter orange hat or cap. (Exception: waterfowl hunters in a blind or boat and raccoon hunters at night.)

MICHIGAN All firearm hunters on any land during daylight hunting hours must wear a hat, cap, vest, jacket, rainwear, or other outer garment of hunter orange visible from all sides. All hunters, including archers, must comply during gun season. Camouflage hunter orange is legal provided 50 percent of the surface area is **solid** hunter orange. (Exception: Waterfowl, crow, and wild turkey hunters, and bow hunters for deer during open archery season.)

MINNESOTA A person may not hunt or trap during the open season in a zone or area where deer may be taken by firearms, unless the visible portion of the person's cap or outer clothing above the waist, excluding sleeves and gloves, is blaze orange within each square foot. Blaze orange includes a camouflage pattern of at least 50 percent blaze orange with each square foot. The commissioner may, by rule, prescribe an alternative color in cases where blaze orange would violate the Religious Freedom Restoration Act of 1993, public law number 103-141.

MISSISSIPPI All deer hunters during any gun season must wear in full view at least 500 square inches of **solid,** unbroken hunter orange visible from all sides.

MISSOURI During firearm deer season, all hunters must wear a cap or hat and a shirt, vest, or coat having the outermost color be hunter orange and must be plainly visible from all sides while being worn. Camouflage orange garments do not meet this requirement. (Exception: Department of Conservation areas where deer hunting is restricted to archery methods.)

MONTANA All big-game hunters and those accompanying them must wear at least 400 square inches of hunter orange above the waist. A hat or cap alone is not sufficient. (Exception: bow hunters during special archery season.)

NEBRASKA All deer, antelope, or elk hunters with firearms must wear at least 400 square inches of hunter orange on the head, back, and chest. Upland game hunters are strongly recommended to wear hunter orange.

NEVADA Upland and big-game hunters are strongly recommended to wear hunter orange.

NEW HAMPSHIRE Upland and big-game hunters are strongly recommended to wear hunter orange.

NEW JERSEY All hunters with firearms for deer, rabbit, hare, squirrel, fox, or game birds must wear a cap of **solid** hunter orange or other outer garment with at least 200 square inches of hunter orange visible from all sides. (Exception: waterfowl, wild turkey, and bow hunters.)

NEW MEXICO Upland and big-game hunters are strongly recommended to wear hunter orange.

NEW YORK Upland and big-game hunters are strongly recommended to wear hunter orange.

NORTH CAROLINA Any person hunting game animals other than foxes, bobcats, raccoons, and opossums, or hunting upland game birds other than wild turkeys, with the use of firearms, must wear a cap or hat on his head made of hunter orange materials or an outer garment of hunter orange, visible from all sides. (Exception: landowners hunting on their own land.)

NORTH DAKOTA Every person, while hunting big game, shall wear a head covering and an outer garment above the waistline, both of daylight fluorescent orange color, totaling 400 square inches or more and both to be worn conspicuously on the person. This section does not apply to any person hunting big game with bow and arrow during special bow hunting seasons. Additionally, while the muzzle-loader and the deer gun seasons are in progress in an area, all big-game hunters, including bow hunters, are required to wear a head covering and an outer garment above the waistline of **solid** daylight fluorescent orange color, totaling at least 400 square inches.

OHIO All deer hunters during gun deer seasons must wear a visible hunter orange hat, cap, vest, or coat.

OKLAHOMA All firearm deer hunters must wear a head covering and outer garment above the waist with at least 500 square inches of clothing of which 400 square inches must be hunter orange. All other hunters must wear either a head covering or outer garment of hunter orange during open gun deer season. (Exception: waterfowl, crow, or crane hunters, and those hunting fur-bearing animals at night.)

OREGON Upland and big-game hunters are strongly recommended to wear hunter orange.

PENNSYLVANIA All fall small game, turkey, bear and deer hunters during the regular firearm deer season, and special archery deer season hunters during any portion of the archery season that coincides with the general small game or turkey seasons, must wear at least 250 square inches of hunter orange material on the head, chest and back combined. Spring turkey hunters must wear a minimum of 100 square inches of hunter orange on the head or back and chest while moving from one location to another. Groundhog hunters must wear 100 square inches of hunter orange on the head. *All* required hunter orange must be visible in a 360 degree arc. (Exceptions: waterfowl, mourning dove, crow, flintlock deer season, and archery season hunters except as specified.)

RHODE ISLAND Statewide, October 17–February 28 all hunters, unless bow hunting, hunting raccoon or fox at night, and waterfowl hunting as provided, must wear an outer garment consisting of a minimum of 200 square inches of **solid** daylight fluorescent hunter orange material worn above the waist, and visible in all directions. This may be a hat and/or vest. Statewide, during shotgun season for deer, all hunters, except waterfowl hunters as provided, must wear an outer garment containing a minimum of 500 square inches of

solid daylight fluorescent hunter orange material, worn above the waist visible from all directions and must include a head covering. (Exceptions: during muzzle-loading season all hunters must wear 200 square inches as stated above.) State management areas: October 17–February 28 all users, except as otherwise provided and except users of boat launching sites, must wear at least 200 square inches of **solid** daylight fluorescent hunter orange material as defined above.

SOUTH CAROLINA On all WMA lands and lands within the Central Piedmont, Western Piedmont, and Mountain Hunt units during the gun hunting season for deer, all hunters must wear either a hat, coat, or vest of **solid** visible international orange. Hunters are exempt from this requirement while hunting for dove, duck, and turkey. Small-game hunters while hunting at night or on privately owned lands within the hunt unit are also exempt.

SOUTH DAKOTA All big-game hunters with firearms must wear one or more exterior hunter orange garments above the waist. (Exception: turkey hunters.)

TENNESSEE All big-game hunters with firearms must wear at least 500 square inches of hunter orange on a head covering and an outer garment above the waist, visible front and back. (Exception: turkey hunters during gun hunts proclaimed by the commission and those hunting on their own property.)

TEXAS All hunters and persons accompanying a hunter on national forests and grasslands must wear a minimum of 144 square inches of hunter orange visible on both the chest and back plus a hunter orange cap or hat. Call the U.S. Forest Service and the U.S. Army Corps of Engineers for more information.

UTAH A person shall wear a minimum of 400 square inches of hunter orange material while hunting any species of big game. Hunter orange material must be worn on the head, chest, and back. A camouflage pattern in hunter orange does not meet the requirements of Subsection (1)(a). A person is not required to wear hunter orange material during an archery, muzzle-loader, or big horn sheep hunt unless a centerfire rifle hunt is in progress in the same area.

VERMONT Upland and big-game hunters are strongly recommended to wear hunter orange.

VIRGINIA Hunters during firearm deer season and those accompanying them must wear hunter orange on the upper body, visible from all sides, or a hunter orange hat, or display 100 square inches of hunter orange within body reach, at shoulder level, or higher, visible from all sides.

WASHINGTON All hunters must wear fluorescent hunter orange clothing with a minimum of 400 square inches of fluorescent hunter orange exterior, worn above the waist and visible from all sides. (Exception: Persons who are hunting upland game birds during an upland game bird season with a muzzle-loading firearm, bow and arrow, or falconry.)

WEST VIRGINIA All deer hunters during deer gun season must wear at least 400 square inches of hunter orange on an outer garment.

WISCONSIN All hunters during gun deer season must have 50 percent of their outer garments above the waist, including any head covering, colored hunter orange. (Exception: waterfowl hunters.)

WYOMING All big-game hunters must wear one or more exterior garments (i.e., hat, shirt, jacket, coat, vest, or sweater) of hunter orange. (Exception: bow hunters during special archery season.)

CANADA

ALBERTA No garment color requirements or recommendations.

BRITISH COLUMBIA No garment color requirements or recommendations.

MANITOBA A solid blaze orange hat and an additional 2,580 square centimeters of blaze orange above the waist and visible from all sides must be worn by big-game hunters. Bow hunters are exempt during bow hunting seasons or in bow hunting areas only. Wolf hunters are exempt when hunting in game hunting areas while no other big game season is on. Black bear and wolf hunters are exempt during the spring season.

NEW BRUNSWICK Every person, while hunting or being a licensed guide accompanying any person engaged in hunting, shall wear a hat and upon his or her back, chest, and shoulders an exterior garment of which not less than 2,580 square centimeters in aggregate shall be exposed to view in such a manner as to be plainly visible from all directions, and the color of the hat and the exterior garment shall be solid hunter orange.

NEWFOUNDLAND AND LABRADOR Upland and big-game hunters are strongly recommended to wear a minimum of 2,580 square centimeters of hunter orange (400 square inches).

NORTHWEST TERRITORIES Upland and big-game hunters are strongly recommended to wear hunter orange.

NOVA SCOTIA All hunters and those accompanying them must wear a cap or hat and a vest, coat, or shirt of solid hunter orange visible from all sides. Camouflage hunter orange is permitted during bow hunter season for deer as long as there are at least 400 square inches visible from all sides.

ONTARIO Upland and big-game hunters are strongly recommended to wear a minimum of 2,580 square centimeters of hunter orange (400 square inches).

PRINCE EDWARD ISLAND All upland game hunters are encouraged to wear hunter orange.

QUEBEC All hunters, guides, and companions must wear at least 2,580 square centimeters (400 square inches) of hunter orange on their back, shoulders, and chest, visible from any angle. During hunting season through December 1, coyote, fox, and wolf hunters and guides are required to wear the same as other hunters. (Exceptions: crow or migratory bird hunters and those hunting deer or moose during special archery seasons.)

SASKATCHEWAN All big-game hunters must wear a complete outer suit of scarlet, bright yellow, hunter orange or white, and a head covering of any of these colors except white. (Exception: bow hunters and black powder hunters during special archery muzzle-loading seasons.)

YUKON No garment color requirements or recommendations.

Note: **Maryland, Michigan, Minnesota**, and **Wisconsin** require 50 percent of a camouflage hunter orange garment be open hunter orange.

Maryland requires 50 percent of camouflage hunter orange garment to be daylight fluorescent orange color.

Nova Scotia refuses to recognize camouflage hunter orange as a legal fabric except during archery deer season.

Wisconsin accepts camouflage orange, though solid hunter orange is recommended.

The IHEA recommends the description of hunter orange as "having a dominant wavelength between 595 and 605 nanometers, a luminance factor of not less than 40 percent, and an excitation purity of not less than 85 percent." Highland guarantees that Ten Mile Cloth, Camo Ten, Easy Ten, and TenAcious meet these specifications.

With the now widespread use of hunter orange, some hunters may be tempted to assume that anything that is not orange is not human. Nothing could be more dangerous. Not everyone in the woods is a hunter, and not every hunter is going to be wearing hunter orange.

Every hunter wants to be successful, to get a deer, elk or antelope, to come home with a nice brace of pheasant or grouse. In good measure, that's what hunting is all about. The younger and less experienced we are, the more emphasis we place on being "successful," and that's natural. As the seasons go by, for most of us, this aspect of hunting becomes less important; but when we're in the field, it's still easy to become excited and more than a little bit anxious when we sense that game is nearby. Is that a buck? a doe? just a noisy squirrel? We hold our breath. All our senses come alive, and the seconds of waiting seem to turn into minutes. Will we get a shot or not?

Novice or veteran, it's during moments such as these—the sometimes split second when we must decide to pull the trigger or hold up—that **we must consciously make sure our emotions don't override our good judgment.**

Not all mistaken-for-game accidents are caused by "early blur." All too often, the prime contributing factor is the overeager and overanxious attitude on the part of some hunter. They are typically the kinds who enter the woods determined not to come home empty-handed. Already primed, they need but a small catalyst—a sound or movement in the brush, a spot of color—to shoulder the gun and fire.

Hunting is not a competitive sport. At the end of the day, there are no winners or losers. Sure, there are moments of high excitement and anticipation; what would hunting be without them? And that's exactly why emotional control and mental discipline are essential to safe hunting. Whatever the situation, your decision to shoot must be deliberate and thoughtful. In hunting, there's simply no room for snap judgments. Once you pull the trigger, you can never call that shot back.

In any circumstances where there might be a possibility of mistaking a human being for a game animal, you should take care to:

- Always assume that any movement or sound is another person—not a game animal. **Never shoot at a sound or movement.**
- Never hurry a shot. If you have even the slightest doubt about the identity of your target, hold up. Glance away and then look back. Try to get a view from a different angle. If you have to move, do so. It is far better to spook an animal than to risk an unsafe shot.
- Be doubly cautious during the poor light conditions of dawn and dusk or when the weather has restricted visibility. Such times and conditions are especially conducive to "early blur."
- Take into account that your emotions may be running in high gear. Don't allow your imagination to take over, and don't anticipate a shot. Keep reminding yourself that all you should be concentrating on is to clearly identify your target.
- No matter how tempting, never risk a shot when you can identify only a part of the animal. **The only time you should shoot is when your target is fully and clearly visible.**

Line-of-Fire Accidents

G OOD JUDGMENT—knowing whether it's safe to shoot or not—is the critical issue not only in mistaken-for-game accidents but also in those cases where the victim was out of sight of the shooter, was covered by a shooter swinging on game, or moved into the line of fire. These are among the most common types of accidents that occur each season throughout the country.

Not every accident can be wholly attributed to a single cause. Often, several contributing factors are involved. Careless positioning or careless movement in the field together with poor shooting judgment are a particularly dangerous combination. Time and again, they literally set the stage for a tragic incident. Here again are some verbatim accident summaries:

- Victim struck in head when party members shot at a deer crossing a road; all were on the gravel road.
- Victim and shooter on stands during a deer drive. Shooter fired at a deer between them. Hit victim 310 feet away.
- Victim struck by a bullet fired down a roadway at a deer crossing the road; victim was over 370 yards away.
- Victim struck by a slug fired at a deer by a party member 545 feet from victim; victim out of sight.
- Victim was hunting with a group of friends. A group of doves came in low, and the party opened fire at the birds. Victim was struck over the right eye by a single birdshot-size pellet.
- Shooter swinging on bird shot victim standing in brush.
- Neither subject could see each other when hunter A fired at a rabbit. Hunter B suffered gunshot wounds to the right leg.

- Hunters were in thick cover and underbrush. Shooter fired at a deer not knowing for sure where his partner was. Victim received gunshot wound to the right hip.
- Shooter shot at rabbit and killed same that was running on top of a little hill. Victim was standing on opposite side of hill completely obscured from shooter's view. BBs went through grass and hit victim in head.
- Victim and shooter were hunting along a state road approximately 300 yards apart. Shooter saw deer and fired three shots. One pellet from the last shot struck the victim in the head.
- Shooter shot at deer. He did not notice his father standing beyond the deer and the father was shot.
- Victim and shooter were riding in a Jeep with two other people. Shooter was shooting at a rabbit, victim jumped out of Jeep as shot was fired. Victim was shot in the back of the head.
- Shooter shot deer down; deer got up and started to run. Shooter shot again, hitting victim (his father) beyond the target.
- Dogs jumped a deer; someone yelled, "It's a buck!" The shooter fired, went over to his target and found victim lying face down in the water at the edge of a lake.

There is a distressing similarity to practically all of these accidents. In the vast majority of cases, the incident could have been avoided if only those involved had better organized and planned their hunt. Whatever hunting technique you and your partner(s) use—whether it involves stationary positions or some kind of drive—it is absolutely essential that you **develop a safe strategy before you head out, and stay with that strategy throughout the hunt.** The larger your party, the more important this becomes.

Of course, part of every effective hunting strategy involves positioning hunters in a way that will maximize their chances of getting a shot at game. Yet the primary objective of every hunting plan must be safety: Establishing clear and well-defined zones of fire is critical. Remember, most line-of-fire accidents involve members of the same hunting party. It bears repeating again: **You can't know what is your safe zone of fire unless you know the location of all your hunting partners.** So, never change your location or line of travel without letting your partners know. Hunter orange clothing not only helps in avoiding the risk of being mistaken for

Always plan your hunt with safety as your primary objective. Develop a safe strategy before you head out, and stay with that strategy throughout the hunt.

game but is also a great aid in helping you keep track of everyone in your group.

In many hunting situations, the direction of fire is predictable and should be taken into account when positioning yourself and your partners. Extreme caution should be taken when placement puts all of you in a likely line of fire. For example, you and your partners hope to get a shot at deer as they cross over a power line cut or abandoned logging road. Everyone wants the opportunity for a clear shot and selects stands along the edge of the road or cut. Even though your positions may be many yards apart, keep in mind that any deer that passes through the line will present a shot that places one—or all of you—in the direct line of fire. The same logic applies when driving deer to standers. Drives require careful planning and execution. There should never be any confusion about the line of travel or the location of both drivers and standers. Accidents in which the victim was out of sight happen all too often during drives for deer.

Any time that you and your hunting partners are walking, make every possible effort to stay in your agreed-upon position, especially when game is nearby. Hunters who move around too much, who

Never take a shot unless you know what lies in the area beyond your target. What's behind this pronghorn antelope? Who knows?

"break formation," can easily lose track of one another. If at any moment you're not sure where your partner is, don't hesitate to call out. Extra caution should be taken when moving through heavy cover. When you and your partner(s) can't see one another, stay in verbal contact.

In any hunting situation, you not only must be sure that your target is fully and clearly visible but you must also know what lies in the area beyond your target. **Never shoot unless you're positive that you have a safe background.** Whether you're using a rifle or shotgun, never forget that the bullet or shot charge can travel well beyond your target. And be especially careful when taking a second or third shot at flying or running game. In a moment of excitement, it's easy to get carried away and swing beyond your safe zone of fire.

Accidents that involve a hunter's judgment, whether mistaken-for-game or line-of-fire, account for almost half of all accidents that occur each year. Accidents of this type also account for a disproportionately large number of fatalities. Whether you're a novice or a veteran of many seasons, you should:

Never hurry or anticipate a shot. If you have the slightest doubt, hold up.

- Always wear hunter orange outerwear, if appropriate for your kind of hunting.
- Never assume that if something is not orange it's not human.
- Never wear or carry anything that resembles a game animal.
- Always assume that any unidentified sound or movement is another human being—not a game animal.
- Always try to maintain the right attitude toward hunting. Never overemphasize the importance of being "successful."
- Never allow your emotions to override your good judgment. Mental discipline is critical to safe hunting.
- Never hurry or anticipate a shot. If you have the *slightest* doubt, hold up. Never use your rifle scope as a pair of binoculars.
- Always be doubly cautious about taking a shot during the poor light conditions of dawn or dusk or when the weather has restricted visibility.

- Never risk a shot when you can identify only part of an animal. The only time you should shoot is when your target is fully and clearly visible.
- Always plan your hunt with safety as your primary objective.
- Always be sure you know your safe zone of fire, and never take a shot outside your zone.
- Always know the location of your hunting partners—at all times.
- Always stay in your agreed-upon position when hunting with partners, especially when moving through heavy cover.
- Never take a shot unless you know what lies beyond your target.
- Drag, never carry, your deer out of the woods.

CHAPTER

Special Considerations: Turkey and Waterfowl Hunting

TURKEY-HUNTING SAFETY

A true native species, the wild turkey originally ranged throughout most all regions of the North American continent. However, by the 1930s encroaching civilization and subsistence hunting had reduced populations to a point where the future of the species was in doubt. Only small and scattered flocks, mostly in the Deep South, remained.

Efforts by wildlife managers to restore the turkey have been nothing short of spectacular. In just some 50 years, restocking programs have brought wild turkey back to 44 states, including some places where the bird was not found in the days of the Indians. Today, 49 states offer spring turkey hunting, and 39 states have a full turkey season. Since turkey hunting is still new to many hunters, it's well worth looking at the specific safety issues that apply when hunting this challenging bird.

At first glance, the very nature of turkey hunting may appear to encourage mistaken-for-game accidents. Consider: When hunting turkey you are (1) typically wearing camouflage clothing; (2) in a well-concealed position; (3) using a call to imitate "turkey talk."

Actually, turkey hunting should be among the safest types of hunting. Knowledgeable turkey hunters, those who hunt in a sport-

74

ing and ethical fashion by calling birds in to a point where a clean kill is assured, are rarely, if ever, the cause of turkey-hunting accidents. Ironically, however, they are most often the victims.

An analysis of turkey-hunting accidents reveals that in the vast majority of cases the shooter stalked his victim, and the shooter thought he was shooting at a calling turkey.

Ethical standards and knowledge of game can play an important role in hunting safety. Hunters, for example, who try to stalk a bird often lack not only a basic understanding of turkey hunting but of turkeys as well. New York state game officials point out that the only legal turkeys in the spring are those with beards. During the spring season, a caller is imitating the call of a hen—not a tom. There is no resemblance between the yelp of a hen and the gobbling of a male. Why, then, would anyone try to sneak up to a calling hen? Some hunters simply don't know any better. Others may choose to ignore the fact. In either case, an accident can easily result.

What about the use of hunter orange for turkey hunters? Frankly, the issue is still being debated. Accident statistics indicate that this safety color may not be the answer. Victims in most accidents were wearing some sort of contrasting colors—usually red, white, or blue; and in one reported case hunter orange gloves. Apparently, such colors are easily mistaken for the tom turkey's colorful head. Hunters in full camouflage gear—the standard for most turkey hunters—were involved in far fewer accidents.

All hunters have an obligation to become familiar with the hunting methods that are appropriate for the game they hunt and to become knowledgeable about the species' habits and characteristics. Every turkey hunter should also be aware of the safety rules that specifically apply to turkey hunting developed by the National Wild Turkey Federation:

1. Don't ever attempt to approach closer than 100 yards to a hen or a gobbler.
2. Never select a calling site with your back to a tree that is smaller than the width of your shoulders.
3. Never jump and turn suddenly because you hear a turkey close behind you.
4. Never select a calling site where you can't see at least 40 yards in all directions.
5. Never stalk a turkey.

Never presume that what
you hear or what answers
you is a turkey.

6. Don't use a gobbler call unless it's one of those rare situations
   where circumstances really warrant trying something different.
7. Don't think because you're fully camouflaged that you're
   totally invisible.
8. Never wear red, white or blue clothing, not even undergar-
   ments of these colors.
9. Never presume that what you hear or what answers you is a
   turkey.
10. Don't try to hide so well that you can't see what's happening.

WATERFOWL AND BOATING SAFETY

Waterfowlers are a different breed of hunter. At a time when most
upland gunners have called it a season, the duck and goose hunter is
in full swing, waiting for winter's worst and the chance to break skim
ice at 5 A.M. on a day when the clouds are low and the wind is up. But
more than just weather or the time of year, waterfowling involves
some special safety considerations.

First, in most waterfowling situations you will be shooting within a few feet of your partners. So, whether you're hunting from a
boat, pit, or blind, **the need for precisely defined and religiously
adhered to zones of fire is of paramount importance.** Establishing zones of fire should always be the first thing you and your
partners decide on, even before loading up.

In some situations, it's best if only one gunner fires at a time.

A boat is no place for a loaded gun. Guns should be unloaded, with the action open, when getting in or out of a boat.

Some boats and blinds, for example, are simply too small and cramped to allow two, or more, gunners to shoot at once. If that's the case, **be sure that everybody knows the shooting order—and sticks with it.** As a reminder, each shot should be called in advance, "It's your shot, Joe." A classic waterfowling accident involves two hunters getting up simultaneously, each thinking the shot is "his." All too often, one hunter ends up in the direct line of fire of the other.

Since boats, pits, and blinds are confined and often crowded, it's essential that you and your partners know exactly when and in which direction it's safe to shoot.

One of the cardinal rules of safe gun handling is to have control of your gun at all times. When duck and goose hunting, this typically involves having your shotgun in a secure rest with the muzzle pointing in a safe direction. For instance, never simply prop your gun up with the barrel resting against the side of the blind or pit. Left this way, it could easily slip or be knocked over by an anxious retriever. If there's no secure rest, hold your gun firmly with the muzzle pointing up and away from the boat, blind, and companions.

In the close quarters often experienced when duck and goose hunting, extra caution should also be taken when loading and unloading. In either case, stand up and point the muzzle outside the blind in a safe direction. **Under no circumstance should you try to get in or out of a blind, pit, or boat with a loaded gun.**

Maneuvering inside a blind or pit—and especially in a small boat— is tricky, so be sure to always pay strict attention to where the muzzle of your gun is pointing. Never reach over and pull a shotgun toward you, muzzle first. And when the time comes to pull your boat ashore, be sure your gun is not still in the boat, its muzzle pointing at your back.

While many waterfowlers use boats, not enough waterfowlers think of themselves as "boaters." Instead, boats are often seen as just another piece of gear, something to be hauled out and put into the water a few times each season.

As with any other type of equipment, you should be thoroughly familiar with your boat and know how to handle it in a safe manner. And that's not just pro forma advice: Each season, more hunters die from boating accidents than they do from shooting mishaps. Indeed, sportsmen such as duck and goose hunters are far more likely to be involved in boating accidents than the traditional summer boaters.

Boating accident statistics show that most accidents occur "out of season," during the spring and fall months, and typically involve a small boat equipped with either no motor or one of 10 horsepower or less.

Maintaining the stability of a small boat is critical—and doubly so when out in cold waters. No boat should ever be overloaded or over-powered. Check the capacity plate on your boat, and never exceed the craft's maximum ratings for weight or horsepower. And remember, a small boat is no place to stand up. If you do have to change positions, keep a low profile, and keep your weight centered toward the middle of the craft.

Falling out of a boat into cold water is extremely dangerous. Cold water conducts heat from your body some 30 times faster than cold air. Your survival time in near-freezing water is literally a matter of minutes. In fact, hypothermia, the rapid and drastic chilling of the body core, is more often than not the cause of death in victims who fall into cold water.

What should you try to do in case you fall overboard? Try not to panic. The more you thrash around, the faster your body heat will escape. And don't worry about your heavy duck-hunting clothes dragging you under. Actually, by trapping air, they will help you stay afloat and also help preserve body heat. Your number one priority is to get out of the water as fast as you possibly can.

Your chances of making it are greatly increased if you are wearing a personal flotation device (pfd). Just having a pfd in the boat is not enough. Even in mild temperatures, getting into a pfd once you're in the water is tricky. In cold water, the task is next to impossible. Today, there are a wide variety of flotation jackets and vests specifically designed for the waterfowler. If your duck and goose hunting takes you out in a boat, buy one—and wear it. More than any other piece of equipment, it could save your life.

Remember that during the waterfowl season you'll likely be the only "boaters" out on the water. Should something happen, you can't expect help to come quickly, if at all. So being well prepared for an emergency is especially important.

Should you fall overboard when out in cold water, your chances of survival are greatly increased if you are wearing a personal flotation device (pfd). More than any other piece of equipment, a pfd could save your life.

A few other points to be *sure* of:

- Be sure to dress properly. Several layers of light clothing offer better protection than a single heavy layer. And wool retains its insulating properties even when wet.
- Be sure to check the weather forecast before planning your trip, and tell someone where you're going and when you expect to return. When out on the water, be conscious of weather patterns and changes. Don't push your luck. If the wind really picks up and the skies darken, head back in—even though the ducks may be piling into your rig.
- Be sure your boat and motor are in good condition and are adequate for the water conditions you might encounter. On board, be sure to have a bailing device, oars or paddles, a signaling device, and a class B1 fire extinguisher if the boat has an inboard engine or built-in gas tanks.
- Be sure never to overload your boat. An overloaded boat can easily capsize, even in calm conditions.
- Be sure to **always wear a personal flotation device.**

CHAPTER

Alcohol Abuse

NO SANE INDIVIDUALS drive when they have had a few drinks. Nor do sane individuals handle guns after they have had a couple of drinks. Even the normally safety-conscious hunter or shooter becomes an accident just waiting to happen when under the influence of alcohol. Safe gun handling requires coordination, balance, and an alert mind. And every shooting situation involves a judgment call, a decision, often made in a brief second, whether to shoot or hold up. Alcohol depresses brain functions. As a result, it takes us longer to process information, and still more time to react. What's more, alcohol affects focus and depth perception and makes it difficult to judge speed correctly or track moving objects. And finally, alcohol reduces inhibitions, causing normally cautious individuals to try stunts they would avoid when sober. This is especially true of inexperienced drinkers.

To be sure, alcohol affects everyone differently, depending on factors such as body size, drinking experience, and the amount of food in the stomach. But whether you're an experienced drinker or not, the point to remember is that alcohol can seriously jeopardize the safety of everyone in your hunting party.

Consider these facts:

- Beer or wine is not less intoxicating than hard liquor. One 12-ounce can of beer contains the same amount of alcohol as 4 ounces of wine or 1½ ounces of 86 proof liquor.
- Alcohol enters the bloodstream immediately. It takes 1½ hours for a 12-ounce beer to leave the body of an average-size adult. A cold shower, coffee, or fresh air will not help you sober up.
- Alcohol does not warm you up. In small amounts, it does dilate

the small blood vessels close to the skin and give a deceptive "glow" of warmth. However, dilated blood vessels reduce your body's ability to guard against heat loss.

If you use a boat when hunting, you should also be aware that alcohol is by far the number one killer on the water. Alcohol is the major contributing factor in as many as 70 percent of all boating deaths.

Most boating fatalities are caused by an accidental fall out of the boat. Balance and coordination are among the first things affected by drinking. Once in the water, even an able swimmer can easily drown. And with alcohol in the blood, the numbing effects of cold water occur much faster than when you're sober.

Drinking when handling a gun, or a boat or an automobile, for that matter, is not only an invitation to disaster but also against the law. If you do drink, save the cocktail hour for the fireside stories when you get home in the evening.

CHAPTER

Muzzle-Loading Safety

EVEN THOUGH OBSOLETE for more than three-quarters of a century, the use of muzzle-loading rifles, shotguns, and handguns is currently enjoying an enormous revival. Today, there are more than 3 million muzzle-loading enthusiasts throughout the country, both hunters and target shooters. In fact, most states now have a muzzle-loading-only big-game season.

The National Muzzle Loading Rifle Association, Box 67, Friendship, Indiana 47201, provides shooting news, safety and handling hints, and a wealth of technical information for black-powder shooters. The following safety information is provided courtesy of the NMLRA.

Powder

Use only black powder or the proper grade of pyrodex in all muzzle-loading firearms. Pyrodex is unsuitable for flintlocks. The term *black powder* refers to a type of gunpowder, not a color. If in doubt, don't use it. **Never use smokeless powder in a muzzle-loading firearm.**

Black Powder Types

Fg—The coarsest. Use in big-bore (70-caliber and up) arms, scale-model cannons, and shotguns.

FFg—Use in smooth-bore muskets, in rifles over 45 caliber, and in shotguns.

FFFg—Most common. Use in rifles up to .45 caliber and in all pistols and revolvers.

FFFFg—Finest granulation. Use only for priming flintlocks.

Patches

Use only linen or 100 percent cotton for shooting patches. Fabric should have a hard finish and be tightly woven, between .007 inches and .020 inches thick.

Recommended precut patch sizes

CALIBER	PATCH DIAMETER (INCHES)
.45	1
.50	1⅛
.54	1¼
.58	1⅜

All patches should be lubricated before loading. Use a clean-burning grease or commercial patch lube (such as Hoppes #9, Hodgdon's Spit Patch) or saliva.

Ball or Bullet

The patched round ball is thought to be the most accurate bullet for use in rifled, single-shot muzzle-loading firearms.

Use pure lead only in casting any type of bullets for use in muzzle loaders. Plumber's lead is good. Wheel weights are too hard.

Always use a lubricated cloth patch when using a round ball. And always load a round ball with the sprue up (the sprue is the flat place on the cast round ball).

Ignition Systems

The two most common forms of ignition in contemporary muzzle-loaders are flintlock and percussion. In the flintlock system, a piece of flint strikes a hardened piece of steel (the frizzen), causing a shower of sparks, which in turn ignites a small quantity of powder in the lock pan. This ignites the main charge in the barrel and fires the gun.

In the percussion system, the priming charge is replaced by the percussion cap. This cap is placed on the nipple, or cone. When struck by the hammer, it produces a small, hot flame that ignites the main powder charge. Of the two systems, the caplock is the less complicated and the less susceptible to dampness.

Be sure to check periodically the action of your locks, especially with muzzle-loading shotguns. If performance is doubtful, take them to a gunsmith who is familiar with muzzle-loading firearms. Poor locks are a menace to shooters and spectators alike.

Determining Powder Charges

Since there are many variances among muzzle-loading firearms available in today's market, it is essential that you follow the manufacturer's powder-charge recommendations. If you seek the advice of a reputable dealer or muzzle-loading expert, be sure to bring your firearm with you. He or she will want to see the gun before advising you. Remember, in any muzzle-loading firearm, moderate loads are more accurate.

Loading Procedure for Rifle and Single-Shot Pistol

1. Check that your firearm is empty and unprimed.
2. Put the hammer at half-cock.
3. Run a dry patch through the barrel to remove any remaining oil.
4. When the line is clear to handle firearms, snap a cap or strike a pan of powder to dry the breech.

Never fire a muzzle loader unless the ball or shot charge is firmly seated against the powder charge.

5. Put the butt on the ground between your feet when loading a rifle, with the muzzle away from you.
6. Measure a charge of powder—level full without jarring the measure.
7. Pour the measured charge into the barrel. Tap the side of your barrel with your hand to settle the powder in the breech.
8. Center a lubricated patch on the muzzle.
9. Place a round ball on the patch, sprue up.
10. Drive the patch/ball into the barrel using a short starter (bullet starter).
11. Using the ramrod, press the ball and patch all the way down against the powder charge. Seat them firmly with even pressure.
12. Remove the ramrod.
13. Cap or prime with powder.
14. Aim and fire.

Loading Procedure for Shotgun

1. Check that the shotgun is empty and unprimed.
2. Put the hammer at half cock.
3. Run a dry patch through the barrels to remove any remaining oil.
4. When the line is clear to handle firearms, snap a cap or strike a pan of powder to dry the breech.

5. Put the butt on the ground between your feet with the muzzle away from you.
6. Measure a charge of powder—level full without jarring the measure.
7. Pour the measured charge into the barrel. Tap the side of the barrel with your hand to settle the powder in the breech.
8. Place Nitro card wad over the powder, followed by a wet fiber wad. Seat each wad firmly.
9. Pour the measured shot into the barrel. Equal powder and shot charges by volume work best.
10. Finally, add the overshot card wad. Seat firmly—don't pound down.
11. Remove the ramrod.
12. Cap or prime with powder.
13. Bring the hammer to full cock.
14. Aim and fire.

After firing both barrels, make it a fixed habit always to put hammers at half-cock position to lessen the chance of an accidental discharge. If reloading one barrel while the other barrel is still loaded, **always remove cap** from the nipple of the loaded barrel to prevent accidental discharge of that barrel.

Loading Procedure for Revolver

1. Make sure the revolver is empty and unprimed.
2. Run a dry patch through the barrel and cylinder to remove any remaining oil.
3. When the line is clear to handle firearms, cap each chamber and snap it to make sure every nipple is clear of oil or powder fouling.
4. Pour the measured powder into the chamber.
5. Seat the ball (0.001–0.002 over the cylinder bore diameter) firmly down on the powder. Try to apply the same pressure in loading each chamber.
6. When all are loaded, grease the chambers on top of each ball. Use commercial lubes, Crisco, or a similar substance.
7. Cap the revolver nipples with tight-fitting caps. Choose caps with care. Make sure that they fit well (almost too tight) and

that they break up uniformly and completely when fired rather than merely enlarging.

8. Carefully aim and fire.

As an alternative to grease over the end of each cylinder chamber, you may wish to use a greased or waxed felt wad approximately ⅛-inch thick. This will go on top of the powder charge, under the ball.

Muzzle-Loading Safety Rules

1. Muzzle-loading firearms are not toys. Treat them with the same respect due any firearm.
2. Use only black powder of the proper granulations in your muzzle-loading firearms. Such guns are not designed to withstand the higher pressures developed by modern smokeless powders.
3. Never fire a muzzle loader unless the ball or shot charge is firmly seated against the powder charge. And always make sure that the ball or shot charge is seated against the powder. An air space between the powder and the projectile will cause the barrel to be ringed or bulged and in some cases may cause the barrel to rupture.
4. Do not exceed the manufacturer's recommended maximum loads or attempt to load multiple projectile loads. When in doubt, secure information concerning proper loads from an authoritative source.
5. When loading, do not expose your body to the muzzle. Grasp the ramrod only a short distance above where it protrudes from the barrel, pushing it down in short strokes, rather than grasping it near the outer end, where, in the event the rod breaks, serious injury can be rendered by the shooter's arm coming into contact with the splintered end of the broken rod.
6. Always make sure that your down-range area is a safe impact area for your projectiles. Round balls may carry as far as 800 yards and elongated projectiles well beyond this distance.
7. Never smoke while loading, shooting, or handling black powder.

When shooting a muzzle loader, keep in mind that round balls may carry as far as 800 yards and elongated projectiles well beyond this distance.

8. Do not load directly from a powder horn or flask. Always use a separate measure. A lingering spark in the barrel can ignite the incoming charge, causing the horn or flask to explode in your hand.
9. The half-cock notch is the safety notch on a muzzle loader. Always be sure it is functioning properly. If your lock or triggers seem to be improperly functioning, take your firearm to a competent muzzle-loading gunsmith.
10. Never use 4F black powder as a main charge. It burns too fast and could burst a barrel.

11. When you prime your pan, fill it only one-quarter or one-third full. More powder gives an excessive flash.

12. Never snap a percussion lock. It will often break the tumbler. If you snap a flintlock to adjust or test the flint, never do so with the rifle loaded. Even though the pan is not primed, many rifles will fire from the sparks alone.

13. Always wear eye and ear protection.

14. Treat a misfire or failure to fire as though the gun can fire at any second. Wait at least one minute with gun pointed at the target.

15. Do not use a plastic patch. The ball-to-plastic patch fit is critical. If an improper fit or a sharp jolt occurs, the ball will roll down the barrel, leaving an air gap between the ball and the plastic patch. The ball will then act as an obstruction and will cause serious injury to the firearm and possibly the shooter.

16. The nature of a muzzle-loading firearm requires that you, the shooter, exercise caution and skill in the care, loading, and use of such a firearm. Make certain that you are informed as to the proper steps in such care and use.

Clay-Target Safety, Plinking Safety, and Range Commands

Sporting Clays

Introduced to American shooters in the early 1980s, sporting clays has rapidly become one of America's favorite clay-target sports. Today, more than 3½ million shooters enjoy the sport at some 1,500 sporting-clays courses around the country.

With target presentations at each station that simulate the flight of popular game birds, sporting clays is an ideal "hunter's game" providing not only excellent wingshooting practice but a realistic environment for the new hunter to practice safe gun-handling skills such as a safe carry as squad members walk from station to station through woods or fields.

Not surprisingly, the safety rules that apply to other clay-target games, such as trap and skeet, are also applicable to sporting clays. Always carry your shotgun unloaded with the action open as you walk from station to station, and when arriving at a new station, place your shotgun in the gun rack provided. The only time you should load is when you're in the shooting cage and ready to shoot.

Keep in mind that most sporting-clays targets involve doubles—targets thrown simultaneously or one right after the other. On some doubles, when the pair fly close together, it's possible to break both with one shot. In your excitement, don't forget that you still have an unfired round in your shotgun. When finished at a station, always double check to be absolutely sure that your shotgun is unloaded and that the action is open before you leave the shooting cage.

Trap and Skeet

Accidents at trap and skeet clubs are almost unheard of. A key reason is that gun-club safety has become a practiced ritual, a step-by-step pattern that knowledgeable shooters are always careful to follow.

If you're a new shooter, you'll find that the correct approach to safety on the trap and skeet field has a lot in common with developing good shooting skills. In both cases, the vital ingredient is consistency.

Among top shooters, there is a deliberate effort to break targets at each station in the same way. The manner in which the shotgun is mounted, the angle of the muzzle in relation to the house, foot position, and the like, are all part of a style the shooter attempts to duplicate from one round to the next.

Experienced shooters also coordinate the necessary safety procedures into their movements and actions while on the field. The result is a safe, consistent style that soon becomes second nature to the shooter.

If you are new to clay-target shooting, you may find it helpful to think of safety as a specific series of actions that are duplicated from station to station, from round to round.

When at the club, keep these points in mind:

1. Always be sure the trap boy is safely inside the house before you shoot.
2. Should a delay occur while you are in a shooting position, open your gun, extract the shell, and do not reload until you are ready to resume shooting.
3. Never place your hand over the muzzle or lean a gun against your body. Watch the direction of the muzzle at all times.
4. Always carry your gun unloaded with the action open when you are not in firing position. The only time your gun should be loaded is when you're on station and ready to shoot.
5. Never load more than one shell unless you are shooting doubles.

6. Before you head out to the field, check your vest or shell pouch to be sure you're not carrying shells of a different gauge than the gun you're using.

7. Safeties are not used because your gun should never be loaded until you're ready to fire.

8. In skeet, you should not move to the next station until all squad members have finished shooting. Carry guns open from one station to the next.

9. When shooting trap, your gun should be unloaded and open when changing stations, and when moving from station 5 to 1, you should be sure to walk behind other squad members.

10. When you leave your field, double check to make sure your gun is unloaded and be sure to leave the action open.

11. Always wear eye and ear protection!

When plinking or target shooting, be sure you have a safe backstop. The best backstop is a high dirt bank free of rocks and stones.

Plinking

While plinking may be described as informal target shooting, there's never an excuse for a casual approach to gun safety.

To begin with, always select a site with a safe backstop and a safe background. If shooting clay targets thrown from a hand or portable trap, you'll need a safety zone of at least 300 yards. For handgun and rifle shooting, the best backstop is a high dirt bank free of rocks and stones. Such a backstop provides adequate stopping power and eliminates the danger of ricochets. And remember never to shoot at a hard, flat surface or the surface of water.

Second, it's always a good idea to establish a firing line. When shooting, spectators must be behind the firing line. And when you go down range to change targets, all guns should be unloaded, with the actions open, and placed in a secure rest.

Plinking can provide hours of enjoyment in a relaxed atmosphere; but, as in any situation where firearms are involved, there can be no letdown when it comes adhering to all the rules of safe gun handling.

Range Commands

If you have the opportunity to shoot at a formal range, it will be helpful to be familiar with the standard range officer commands:

"Relay No. ( ) and Match No. ( ) on the firing line. The preparation periods starts now."

"With (No. of rounds you'll be using), load."

"Is the line ready?" (If you're not, notify the range officer.)

"Ready on the left. Ready on the right. Ready on the firing line."

"Commence firing."

"Cease firing."

"Unload—actions open, magazines out—guns on the table."

Eye and Ear Protection

IF YOU'VE EVER HEARD ringing in your ears after shooting, it's a clear signal that you've subjected yourself to potentially damaging sound levels. Numerous sound-level tests have shown conclusively that combined exposure to gunfire can cause gradual hearing damage. While the ringing in your ears may go away, any damage to your hearing is permanent.

The faintest sound most of us can hear is around 1 decibel, a very soft whisper. Normal conversation is 50–70 decibels, and hearing loss will result from continuous exposure to sound levels around 130 decibels. *Most gunfire is louder than this 130-decibel level.*

Peak sound-pressure levels produced, for example, by the firing of various rifles (at the U.S. Army Proving Grounds in Aberdeen, Maryland) were measured at 160 to 172.5 decibels. Industry tests have measured the report of a 12-gauge shotgun at 140 decibels. Handguns and other short-barreled firearms, even those of small caliber, produce an unexpectedly loud and sharp report. While the peak sound-pressure level from a .22 rifle measured out at 130 decibels (the measurement was taken 2 feet to one side of the muzzle), a .22 pistol delivered 153 decibels.

Clearly, the repetitious firing on skeet, trap, and target ranges produces the most damage to your hearing. When at the club or range, there's simply no excuse not to wear some type of effective hearing protection. There is a wide variety of hearing protectors available today, from foam plugs and custom molded inserts, to ear-muff devices. Choose the type you find most comfortable—and always use them.

Hearing loss caused by exposure to loud noise is typically a gradual process. As nerve endings in the inner ear are destroyed, certain

Your eyes and ears are irreplaceable. Always wear eye and ear protection when at the range.

sounds can no longer be heard. At first, you may not notice any impairment. But when you do, it's too late. Any hearing damage that's been caused is permanent. No medical or surgical treatment can restore it.

Your eyes, like your ears, are irreplaceable, and there's not a shooting situation in which a pair of high-quality, impact-resistant shooting glasses won't offer an important measure of safety. Most critically, perhaps, shooting glasses can protect you from injury in the unlikely event of a ruptured case or firearm malfunction. In the field, shooting glasses will protect your eyes should you accidentally walk into a sharp twig or get hit in the face by a swinging branch. In such cases, your glasses can prevent what might have been a serious injury or head off the discomfort of an irritated eye that could bring an early end to your hunt. When there are a number of shooters afield, such as during a dove hunt, glasses will also protect your eyes from falling shot. And shooting glasses are an absolute must at the trap and skeet range, where flying clay-target chips and shards can pose a serious hazard to your eyes.

CHAPTER

Reloading Safety

THE OLD SAYING that one person's trash is another's treasure certainly rings true when it comes to a shotshell hull. Left scattered about a trap or skeet field by some shooters, it is—for the reloader—a valued component of a rewarding and money-saving hobby. Beyond the economics, there's an undeniable satisfaction in breaking clay targets or downing game with your "own" loads.

For the rifle and pistol shooter, reloading not only offers savings but also the ability to custom "tune" ammunition to a particular gun and to a specific purpose, whether for target or hunting use.

There's nothing complicated or difficult about reloading, yet it is not something you should attempt until you're familiar with the basic rules of reloading safety.

1. To begin with, reload only when you can give your undivided attention. It's best to develop a reloading routine, and to always load at an unhurried pace.
2. Always wear safety glasses when reloading.
3. If you're new to reloading, take the time to carefully review the introduction section of your loading manual or guide.
4. Again, if you're just starting out, do not reload without an instruction manual for the machine you're using. Take your time and follow the step-by-step instructions. Use your reloading equipment only as the manufacturer recommends.
5. Observe good housekeeping rules in your reloading area. Clean up spilled powder and primers promptly and completely.
6. Store powder and primers beyond the reach of children and away from heat and open flames. Keep no more powder than needed in an open container. Immediately return unused powder to its original factory container. This will preserve its identity and shelf life. Do not store primers in bulk. Primers in bulk can explode spontaneously. Storage areas containing only primers are recommended. These cabinets should be ruggedly constructed of lumber at least 1 inch (nominal) thick to delay or minimize the transmission of heat in the event of fire. Do not store primers with propellant powders or other highly combustible materials. Store primers only in their original factory containers. The use of glass bottles, fruit jars, and plastic and metal containers is extremely hazardous. Take care in filling and handling auto-primer feed tubes.
7. Reload only according to data published in recognized reloading manuals. Never exceed recommended loads, and never use the heaviest recommended powder charge until lighter charges of the same powder have been tried and found safe in each individual gun. Before you start loading, take a second look at the manufacturer's reloading data, which instructs you to use a particular set of components.
8. Do not use any powder unless its identity is positively known. Scrap all mixed powders and those of uncertain or unknown identity.
9. Do not smoke while reloading, and keep a fire extinguisher within reach of your reloading bench.

10. Use priming tools and accessories precisely as the manufacturer recommends. Do not make alterations, substitutions, or changes to priming tools, systems, or accessories.

11. Keep accurate and complete records of your reloads, and be sure to label each box of shells and cartridges.

Firearms Safety in the Home

SOME HUNTERS may think of safety as largely a matter of proper gun handling in the field, but safety in the home is equally important. Indeed, National Safety Council figures reveal that about twice as many firearms accidents occur in the home as outdoors.

There's nothing complicated about gun safety in the home, but beyond the basic safety precautions is the equally important need to maintain a serious attitude when handling firearms. Guns are not toys and should never be treated as such by anyone in your household.

As a first step in home firearms safety, double check to make absolutely sure that all your guns are unloaded. More than one veteran shooter has experienced the disturbing sensation of discovering a shell in the chamber of a gun he thought was unloaded.

Even if you're positive a gun is unloaded, you should not handle it, or show it to a friend, without first opening the action and checking again. Among experienced gunners, this is a kind of ritual that is expected whenever a firearm is examined. It's a good habit to get into.

Your next step should be to review your firearms storage facilities. In a nutshell, all guns—rifles, shotguns, handguns—should be kept in secure, locked racks, cabinets, or safes. Locking storage is doubly important if there are children in the household.

Standing a shotgun in the corner behind the kitchen door or keeping a handgun in the desk drawer is not suitable. If secure storage is not available, trigger locks that open with a key or similar add-on safety devices that prevent the action from being operated should

Firearms in the home should be kept in locked racks or cabinets.

be used. Again, if there are children in the household, such locking devices are essential.

For complete safety, all ammunition should be kept under lock and key and in a location separate from your firearms. An extra safety measure, particularly with children present, can be realized by storing ammunition in another room or on a different floor. The objective is to create a situation in which a conscious effort is required to bring firearms and ammunition together.

Most fatal home firearms accidents occur when youngsters—often children who do not live in the home—discover firearms that adults thought were safely hidden or physically inaccessible. As a gun owner, your most important responsibility is ensuring that children cannot encounter firearms in your home. The precautions you take must be completely effective. Anything less invites tragedy.

Along the lines of occasionally checking the batteries in your smoke detectors, it's a good idea to also periodically go through a home firearms safety review, a checklist that all firearms and ammunition are properly stored and secured. Accidents have occurred, for example, when a firearm was lent to a friend and returned to storage while it was still loaded.

Education is important as well. If you have young children in the home, they should clearly understand the following safety advice: (1) Don't go looking for guns, in your house or a friend's house; (2) if you find a gun in your house—or anywhere else—leave it alone. Don't touch it. Don't let anyone else touch it. Tell an adult immediately; (3) even if a gun looks like a toy, don't touch it. Some real guns look like toy guns, so don't take a chance. Tell an adult.

Air guns and BB guns should also never be treated as toys. All shooting should be under adult supervision in a safe location with an appropriate backstop. Indeed, all the rules of safe gun handling are equally applicable when shooting air or BB guns.

Hunter Education Programs

IN THE LATE 1940s and early 1950s, hunter education programs were available in only a handful of states and, for the most part, consisted of short training sessions on gun safety. Today, hunter education courses are offered by every state and all of the Canadian provinces. Programs now include a minimum of 10 hours of instruction and, in addition to the basics of safe gun handling, provide instruction in wildlife identification, field care of game, wildlife-management basics, hunter responsibilities, and, depending on the need in the area, such basic skills as outdoor survival.

The growth and development of hunter education efforts throughout North America is due largely to the work of the National Rifle Association and the International Hunter Education Association. Over the years, the IHEA has made great strides in upgrading curriculums, classroom materials, teaching techniques and in the recruitment and training of volunteer instructors. Currently, some 50,000 volunteer instructors train over 650,000 young hunters in state wildlife agency–sponsored programs.

Hunter education will help make you not only a safer hunter but a more skillful and knowledgeable hunter as well. For first-time hunters, courses are mandatory in all 50 states and nearly all Canadian provinces. For more information, you should contact the Hunter Safety Coordinator in your state or province.

Hunter Education State and Provincial Coordinators

CANADA

ALBERTA

Conservation Education Coordinator
WISE Foundation
14515-122 Avenue
Edmonton, AB T5L 2W4
403/422-2605
Fax: 403/427-5695

BRITISH COLUMBIA

British Columbia Wildlife Federation
Manager, Hunter
Safety Program
Unit 303, 19292 60th Avenue
Surrey, BC V3S 8E5
604/533-2293
Fax: 604/533-1592

MANITOBA

Hunter Safety Coordinator
Department of Natural Resources
Box 44
200 Saulteaux Crescent
Winnipeg, MAN R3J 3W3
204/945-8671
Fax: 204/945-7782

NEW BRUNSWICK

Manager of Development & Public
    Education
Department of Natural Resources &
    Energy
PO Box 6000
Forestry Complex
Regent Street
Fredericton, NB E3B 5H1
506/453-2440
Fax: 506/453-6699

NEWFOUNDLAND AND LABRADOR

Education Coordinator
Inland Fish & Wildlife Division/DNR
Building 810 Pleasantville
PO Box 8700
St. Johns, NF A1B 4J6
709/729-2549
Fax: 709/729-4989

NORTHWEST TERRITORIES

Hunter Safety Program
Government of NWT
600, 5102-50 Avenue
Yellowknife, NWT X1A 3S8
867/920-6401
Fax: 867/873-0293

NOVA SCOTIA

Department of Hunter Education
PO Box 698
1701 Hollis Street
4th Fl-Founders Square
Halifax, NS B3J 2T9
902/424-4445
Fax: 902/424-8116

ONTARIO

Wildlife Section of Fish & Wildlife
    Branch
ONT Ministry of Natural Resources
PO Box 7000
300 Water Street
Peterborough, ONT K9J 8M5
705/755-1992
Fax: 705/755-1957

PRINCE EDWARD ISLAND

Conservation Officer
Fish & Wildlife Department
Div. PO Box 2000
11 Kent Street
Jones Building, 4th Floor
Charlottetown, PEI C1A 7H8
902/368-4683
Fax: 902/368-5830

QUEBEC

Ministère de l'Environnement et de
   la Faune
Direction Générale du Developpe-
   ment durable
675, Boulevard René-Levesque Est.
   29
Boite 64
Québec, QUE G1R 5V7
418/521-3975 ext. 4841
Fax: 418/643-3754

SASKATCHEWAN

Legislation & Hunter Education
Department of Environment and
   Resource Management
3211 Albert Street
Regina, SASK S4S 5W6
306/787-3017
Fax: 306/787-9544

YUKON

Hunter Education Coordinator
Government of Yukon/Renewable
   Resources
PO Box 2703 (R-7)
Whitehorse, YUK Y1A 2C6
403/667-5617
Fax: 403/667-2691

MEXICO

Hunter Education Coordinator
Proteccion de la Fauna
Mexicana A.C.
Apartado Postal 486 Centro
Saltillo Coahvilla, Mexico
841-4-49-97
Fax: 011/52/841/4-49-97

UNITED STATES

ALABAMA

Hunter Education Coordinator
Department of Conservation and
   Natural Resources
Game & Fish Division
64 North Union Street
Montgomery, AL 36130-1457
334/242-3620
Fax: 334/242-3032

ALASKA

Hunter Education Coordinator
Department of Fish & Game
Wildlife Conservation Division
333 Raspberry Road
Anchorage, AK 99518-1599
907/267-2187 or 907/267-2236
Fax: 907/267-2323

ARIZONA

State Hunter Education Coordinator
Arizona Game & Fish Department
2221 West Greenway Road
Phoenix, AZ 85023
602/789-3242
Fax: 602/789-3903

ARKANSAS

Hunter Education Coordinator
Arkansas Game & Fish Commission
#2 Natural Resources Drive
Little Rock, AR 72205
501/223-6377 or 501/223-6414
Fax: 501/223-6414

CALIFORNIA

Hunter Education Administrator of
   Fish & Game
1416 9th Street
Room 1342-1
Sacramento, CA 95814
916/653-9727 or 916/653-1093
Fax: 916/653-3772

COLORADO

Hunter Education Administrator
Division of Wildlife
6060 Broadway
Denver, CO 80216
303/291-7470
Fax: 303/292-1954

CONNECTICUT

Wildlife Director
49 Elm Street
Hartford, CT 06106-5127
860/424-3011
Fax: 860/424-4078

DELAWARE

Hunter Education Coordinator
Ommelanden Hunter Education
   Training Center
Division of Fish & Wildlife
1205 River Road
New Castle, DE 19720
302/323-5336
Fax: 302/323-5335

FLORIDA

Hunter Education Administrator
Game & Fresh Water Fish Com-
   mission
Farris Bryant Building
620 South Meridian Street
Tallahassee, FL 32399-1600
850/413-0085
Fax: 850/413-7989

GEORGIA

Hunter Education Coordinator
DNR/Wildlife Resources Division,
   L.E.
543 Elliott Trail
Mansfield, GA 30055
770/784-3059 or 770/784-3060
Fax: 770/784-3061

HAWAII

Conservation Education Program
   Specialist
H1 Hunter Education Program
1130 North Nimitz Highway #B-299
Honolulu, HI 96817-4521
808/587-0200
Fax: 808/587-0205

IDAHO

Hunter Education Administrator
Fish & Game Department
600 S. Walnut Street
PO Box 25
Boise, ID 83707
208/334-2633
Fax: 208/334-2148

ILLINOIS

Safety Education Administrator
Illinois DNR/Division of Education
524 S. 2nd Street, Room 530
Springfield, IL 62701-1787
217/524-9505
Fax: 217/782-5177

INDIANA

Outdoor Education Officer, DNR
402 W. Washington Street W-255D
Indianapolis, IN 46204
317/232-4010
Fax: 317/232-8035

IOWA

Recreational Safety Coordinator,
   DNR
Wallace State Office Building
Des Moines, IA 50319-0034
515/281-8652
Fax: 515/281-6794

KANSAS

Hunter Education Coordinator
Kansas Department of Wildlife &
   Parks
512 SE 25th Avenue
Pratt, KS 67124
316/672-5911
Fax: 316/672-3013

KENTUCKY

Hunter Education Administrator
Department of Fish & Wildlife
   Resources
Attn: Hunter Education
#1 Game Farm Road
Frankfort, KY 40601
502/564-4762
Fax: 502/564-6508

LOUISIANA

Hunter Education Coordinator
Department of Wildlife & Fisheries
1995 Shreveport Highway
Pineville, LA 71360
318/487-5885
Fax: 318/487-5886

MAINE

Safety Officer
Department Inland Fisheries &
   Wildlife
284 State Street Station 41
Augusta, ME 04333
207/287-5220 or 207/287-5222
Fax: 207/287-9037

MARYLAND

Outdoor Education Division
MD Natural Resources Police
69 Prince George Street
Annapolis, MD 21401
410/974-2040
Fax: 410/974-5647

MASSACHUSETTS

Hunter Education Program/Enforce-
   ment
PO Box 408
Westminster, MA 01473-0408
617/727-3623
Fax: 617/727-7525

MICHIGAN

Hunter Safety Administrator
DNR Law Enforcement Division
Mason Building, 6th Floor
PO Box 30031
Lansing, MI 48909
517/335-3410
Fax: 517/373-6816

MINNESOTA

Hunter Education Coordinator
Department of Natural Resources
500 Lafayette Road, Box 47
St. Paul, MN 55155-4047
612/296-8904
Fax: 612/297-3727

MISSISSIPPI

Hunter Education Administrator
Department of Wildlife, Fisheries &
   Parks
PO Box 451
Jackson, MS 39205-0451
601/364-2192
Fax: 601/364-2239

MISSOURI

Hunter Training Supervisor
Department of Conservation
PO Box 180
2901 W. Truman Boulevard
Jefferson City, MO 65102-0180
573/751-4115
Fax: 573/751-8971

MONTANA

Hunter Education Coordinator
Montana Fish, Wildlife & Parks
1420 E. Sixth Avenue
PO Box 200701
Helena, MT 59620-0701
406/444-4046 or 406/444-3188
Fax: 406/444-4952

NEBRASKA

Hunter Education Coordinator
AK-SAR-BEN Aquarium
21502 West Highway 31
Gretna, NE 68028
402/332-5487
Fax: 402/332-5853

NEVADA

Hunter Safety Coordinator
Division of Wildlife
PO Box 10678
Reno, NV 89520
702/688-1553
Fax: 702/688-2939

NEW HAMPSHIRE

Hunter Education Coordinator
Fish & Game Department
2 Hazan Drive
Concord, NH 03301
603/271-1736
Fax: 603/271-1438

NEW JERSEY

State Hunter Education Administrator
NJ Division of Fish, Game & Wildlife
26 Route 173 West
Hampton, NJ 08827
908/735-7088 or 908/735-6826
Fax: 908/735-5689

NEW MEXICO

Hunter Education Coordinator
Department of Game & Fish
3841 Midway Place NE
Albuquerque, NM 87109
505/841-8888 x719
Fax: 505/841-8834

NEW YORK

Sportsman Education Administrator
Fish & Wildlife/Environmental Conservation
50 Wolf Road
Albany, NY 12233-4800
518/457-2994 or
1-888-HUNT-ED2
Fax: 518-457-0341

NORTH CAROLINA

Hunter Safety Coordinator
Wildlife Resource Comm./Enforce-
    ment Division
512 N. Salisbury Street
Raleigh, NC 27604
919/733-7191
Fax: 919/733-7083

NORTH DAKOTA

Hunter Education Specialist
Game & Fish Department
100 N. Bismarck Expressway
Bismarck, ND 58501
701/328-6316
Fax: 701/328-6352

OHIO

Outdoor Skills Supervisor
Ohio Division of Wildlife
1840 Belcher Drive
Columbus, OH 43224-1329
614/265-6322
Fax: 614/262-1171

OKLAHOMA

Hunter Education Coordinator
Department of Wildlife Conservation
1801 North Lincoln
Oklahoma City, OK 73105-4998
405/522-4572
Fax: 405/521-6898

OREGON

Hunter Education Coordinator
Oregon Department of Fish &
    Wildlife
PO Box 59 (ZIP 97207)
2501 SW 1st Avenue
Portland, OR 97201
503/872-5264 x5355
Fax: 503/872-5276

PENNSYLVANIA

Hunter Education Coordinator
Game Commission/Hunter–Trapper
    Education
2001 Elmerton Avenue
Harrisburg, PA 17110-9797
717/787-7015
Fax: 717/772-0542

RHODE ISLAND

State Hunter Safety Education Coor-
    dinator
Rhode Island Division of Fish &
    Wildlife
4808 Tower Hills Road
Wakefield, RI 02879
401/789-7055 or 401/789-3094
Fax: 401/783-4460

SOUTH CAROLINA

Hunter Education Coordinator
Department of Natural Resources
Rembert C. Dennis Building
1000 Assembly Street, Suite 310
PO Box 167
Columbia, SC 29202
803/734-3999 or 800/277-4301
Fax: 803/734-3962

SOUTH DAKOTA

Hunter Safety Coordinator
Department of Game, Fish & Parks
523 E. Capitol
Foss Building
Pierre, SD 57501-3182
605/773-4506 or 605/773-3630
Fax: 605/773-6245

TENNESSEE

Education Supervisor
Wildlife Resources Agency
PO Box 40747
Nashville,TN 37204
615/781-6538
Fax: 615/781-6543

TEXAS

Hunter Education Coordinator
Texas Parks & Wildlife Department
4200 Smith School Road
Austin,TX 78744
512/389-8140
Fax: 512/389-8042

UTAH

Hunter Education Coordinator
Utah Division of Wildlife Resources
1594 West North Temple, Street.
   2110
PO Box 146301 (Zip 84114-6301)
Salt Lake City, UT 84116
801/538-4726 or 801/538-4727
Fax: 801/538-4892

VERMONT

Hunter Education Coordinator
Department of Fish & Wildlife
103 S. Main Street, 10 S.
Waterbury,VT 05671-0501
802/241-3720 or 802/241-3722
Fax: 802/241-3295

VIRGINIA

Hunter Education Coordinator
Virginia Department of Game &
   Inland Fishing
PO Box 11104
4010 W. Broad Street
Richmond,VA 23230
804/367-1147
Fax: 804/367-6179

WEST VIRGINIA

Hunter Safety Coordinator
DNR/Law Enforcement Section
Capitol Complex Building 3
1900 Kanawha Boulevard E.
Charleston,WV 25305
304/558-2783
Fax: 304/558-1170

WISCONSIN

Hunter Education Administrator
Department of Natural Resources
PO Box 7921
101 S.Webster
Madison,WI 53707
608/266-1317 or 608/266-2143
Fax: 608/266-3696

WYOMING

Hunter Education Coordinator
Game & Fish Department
5400 Bishop Boulevard
Cheyenne,WY 82006
307/777-4531 or 307/777-4538
Fax: 307/777-4610

WASHINGTON

Hunter Education Coordinator
Department of Fish & Wildlife
600 Capitol Way North
Olympia,WA 98501-1091
360/586-1656
Fax: 360/586-1662

Index